# The False Promise of Administrative Reform

## Administrative Reform

*Implementing Quality Control in Welfare*

# The False Promise of Administrative Reform

## *Implementing Quality Control in Welfare*

Evelyn Z. Brodkin

TEMPLE UNIVERSITY PRESS

PHILADELPHIA

HV95
B725
1986

Temple University Press, Philadelphia 19122
Copyright © 1986 by Temple University. All rights reserved
Published 1986
Printed in the United States of America

The paper used in this publication meets the minimum requirements of American National Standard for Information Sciences—Permanence of Paper for Printed Library Materials, ANSI Z39.48-1984

**Library of Congress Cataloging-in-Publication Data**
Brodkin, Evelyn Z.
  The false promise of administrative reform.
  Bibliography: p.
  Includes index.
  1. Public welfare administration—United States.
2. Public welfare administration—Massachusetts.
I. Title.
HV95.B725   1986      351.84'0973      86-5801
ISBN 0-87722-431-5 (alk. paper)

To I. E. B.

# Contents

# Preface

Welfare is in disrepute with political attacks coming from many corners. Criticism extends from the large public bureaucracies accused of sloppy and wasteful administration to policy designs that purportedly encourage dysfunctional behaviors and keep the poor from rising out of poverty. Such critiques are hardly new. Nor is the quest for reform that has accompanied criticism of welfare throughout its troubled history.

Reformers in welfare and other policy areas tend to argue that the changes they propose are required in order to improve the efficiency, accountability, and effectiveness of public programs. The Reagan Administration is only the most recent to champion the causes of eliminating "fraud, waste, and abuse" and bringing "better management" to government. These objectives may be packaged within an ambitious program of policy revision or may be pursued separately under the rubric of administrative reform.

Administrative reform is obviously attractive as a symbol and desirable as a goal. But its political significance extends beyond these simple virtues to its utility as a mechanism for making substantive changes in policy. The experience of administrative welfare reform provides an unusual opportunity to look beyond reform's rhetoric and to examine, in a specific context, the reform process, its consequences, and its political significance.

Administrative reform promised to bring order to the disorder plaguing the welfare system following the growth of the Aid to Families with Dependent Children (AFDC) program in the sixties. Over the course of the seventies, reformers at federal and state levels engaged in a sustained and manifestly successful drive to clean up welfare administration. In this book, I trace the emergence, implementation, and consequences of administrative welfare reform and seek to illuminate the political conflict that occurred under its auspices.

For some, the analysis offered in these pages may be encouraging, suggesting the efficacy of certain types of managerial strategies for influencing lower-level behaviors in a far-flung bureaucracy. For others, this analysis will be disturbing, suggesting the problematic nature of manifestly straightforward administrative activities and the potential for political manipulation of the policy delivery process. For the poor, this analysis probably reaffirms what they already know—that in the unsettled politics of the American welfare state, they cannot count on promises of reform to enhance their position.

Ideas are rarely proprietary. Many of those developed in this book grew out of interchanges with academic colleagues, practitioners, and friends and built on the ideas of other scholars. Michael Lipsky suggested that I look into administrative welfare reform in Massachusetts. He invited me to join an experiment combining policy analysis and poverty law practice at the Legal Services Institute in Boston. There, in an informal seminar, we began to explore welfare issues with a remarkable group of colleagues, among them Gary Bellow, Lance Liebman, Teresa Nelson, Martin Rein, and William Simon. At times, over the two years of our discussions, we were also joined by Betsy Hecker, Duncan Kennedy, Jim Rowan, and Joan Zorza.

These colleagues and others deserve thanks for sharing ideas and information with me in the course of this project. I am especially indebted to Michael Lipsky for his generosity with ideas, criticism, and encouragement. Also, Walter Dean Burnham and Harvey Sapolsky helped to guide this inquiry in its first stage, as a doctoral thesis at MIT. I benefited immeasurably from the insights and arguments of friends and associates who reviewed my work at various stages, among them: Deborah Auger, Charles Cameron, the late Manuel Carballo, Olivia Golden, Russell Hanson, Martin Holmer, Carrie Hunter, Carol Jones, Norma Kriger, David Lax, William Levin, Janet Levine, Gregory Mills, Mark Moore, Katherine Moss, Marc Roberts, James Sebenius, Rashid Shaikh, and Stephen Thomas. My appreciation extends also to those who helped me to produce this book, especially Michael Ames and Candice Hawley, Estelle Krieger, Barbara Headrick, Margaret Mericle, Jenny Taylor, and my colleagues at SUNY StonyBrook who rescued me more than once from the wonders of word processing.

I am grateful to many individuals in the Massachusetts Department of Public Welfare (managers, workers, and clients), the U.S. Department of Health and Human Services, congressional staffs, the legal services community, and elsewhere, in and out of government, who were willing to speak with me, grant me access to information, and trust me with their confidences.

Finally, I wish to acknowledge financial support for portions of this research from the following institutions: The American Association of University Women; the Joint Center for Urban Studies of MIT and Harvard University; Harvard University's Kennedy School of Government, School of Public Health and Interdisciplinary Programs in Health; and the U.S. Department of Health and Human Services.

# The False Promise of
# Administrative Reform
*Implementing Quality Control in Welfare*

# 1

# A Second Route to Welfare Reform

Disputes over the provision of welfare not infrequently overwhelm legislative channels for resolving them. They spilled into the streets in the sixties. And, in the seventies, they became mired in legislative deadlock. Welfare policymaking is such a contentious business, in part because it necessitates settling such unsettling questions as who deserves aid, how much, and on what terms.

Prior resolution of these questions was upset in the wake of an extraordinarily rapid expansion of the American welfare state. Social welfare expenditures grew from $16.4 billion in 1960 to $54.8 billion by 1970. (See Table 1.1.) Participation in Aid to Families with Dependent Children (AFDC), the major family assistance program, surged between 1965 and 1970, with caseloads more than doubling (from 4.3 million to 9.6 million recipients) and costs tripling (from $1.6 to $4.8 billion). (See Table 1.2.) This signaled a "welfare crisis" to those who believed that costs were too high and rising uncontrollably and that social dependency was reaching unacceptable levels. However, there was considerable political support for an enlarged social welfare state, manifested in congressional expansion of entitlements to medical care and food assistance in the early 1970s.[1]

In the midst of this perceived crisis, public officials urgently searched for a legislative response that would address concerns over welfare's growth but at the same time respect continuing political support for an expanded welfare state. Much has been written about the battles over comprehensive welfare reform that were waged at various points throughout the seventies.[2] For the moment, suffice it to say that they all met the same dismal fate in Congress, where conflicting views on welfare issues proved irreconcilable. Neither bargaining, logrolling, compromise, nor other well-known lubricants of the legislative process could forge a voting majority for welfare reform.

3

**Table 1.1**

Federal Social Welfare Expenditures for Public Aid and Social Insurance and as a Percentage of GNP: 1960–1982

|  | 1960 | 1965 | 1970 | 1975 | 1979 | 1982 |
|---|---|---|---|---|---|---|
| Public Aid* |  |  |  |  |  |  |
| Expenditures (in millions) | $2,116.9 | $3,593.9 | $9,648.6 | $27,204.6 | $43,611.5 | $52,401.9 |
| As a Percent of GNP | .8 | .9 | 1.7 | 2.8 | 2.7 | 2.6 |
| Social Insurance† |  |  |  |  |  |  |
| Expenditures (in millions) | $14,307.2 | $21,806.6 | $45,245.6 | $99,715.0 | $163,743.7 | $249,304.2 |
| As a Percent of GNP | 3.8 | 4.1 | 5.5 | 7.9 | 8.0 | 9.8 |
| Total Social Welfare Expenditures‡ | $16,424.1 | $25,400.5 | $54,894.2 | $126,919.6 | $206,355.2 | $301,706.1 |
| As a Percent of GNP | 4.6 | 5.0 | 7.2 | 10.7 | 10.7 | 12.4 |

Source: *Social Security Bulletin*, December 1984, *47* (12), pp. 14–22.
* Public aid includes payments for public assistance under the Social Security Act, Medicaid, social services, supplemental security income, and food stamps.
† Social insurance includes social security, Medicare, railroad and public employees retirement, and workers compensation.
‡ Includes public aid and social insurance.

**Table 1.2**

AFDC Recipients and Benefits Payments: 1960–1981

|  | 1960 | 1965 | 1970 | 1975 | 1977 | 1980 | 1981 |
|---|---|---|---|---|---|---|---|
| Recipients (in thousands) | 3,073 | 4,396 | 9,659 | 11,404 | 10,796 | 11,101 | 11,199* |
| Payments (in millions) | $1,001 | $1,660 | $4,853 | $9,211 | $10,603 | $12,475 | $12,981 |

Source: *Social Security Bulletin*, June 1985 *48*: 6.
* Averaged over 19 months.

Crisis notwithstanding, policy politics (the politics of what policy should be)[3] seemed stalemated.

The central argument of this book is that administrative reform constituted an alternative to legislative means of responding to the welfare explosion of the sixties. It was an alternative that largely avoided the legislative process, appealed to divergent interests, and lacked obvious political content. Nevertheless, it appears to have produced systematic policy effects that gradually transformed de jure social welfare entitlements into de facto restrictions on the provision of welfare. This transformation was generally unnoticed and unopposed because it occurred as the by-product of manifestly desirable "improvements" in welfare delivery and the apparently uncoordinated activities of thousands of street-level bureaucrats in hundreds of local welfare offices. Irrespective of one's views on whether welfare should have been restricted, administrative welfare reform merits close scrutiny for what it reveals about how this essentially political choice was converted into nonpolitical form. More broadly, it raises questions both about the theoretical implications of transforming policy politics into administrative form and about the pursuit of administrative accountability in public programs.

Little scholarly attention has been paid to the administrative reforms of the seventies, although they may have constituted the most significant welfare reform of that decade. It is hardly surprising that widely publicized battles over comprehensive statutory change would attract more attention than efforts to achieve "better management," "efficiency," or "accuracy" in welfare. As Martin Anderson succinctly states: "Administration is perhaps the most unexciting, intractable area in which to initiate welfare reform. People's eyes glaze over at the first mention of reorganization, revised regulations, and improved personnel administration" (Anderson, 1978, p. 164).[4]

Nevertheless, such mundane activities are important because relatively modest alterations in administrative routines that are incremental and manifestly nonpolitical may produce substantive changes in policy-as-delivered.[5] Ironically, it is in part because administrative reform is hardly the stuff of which political battles are made that it could be effective as a means of initiating policy change.

## Welfare: A History of Conflict and Complexity

An alternative to legislative means of responding to the welfare crisis might have been unnecessary if the issues it raised were more amenable to political resolution. However, opposing views of welfare's fundamental purposes and principles virtually defied reconciliation both because of the nature of these differences (discussed in this chapter) and because of weaknesses in institutional means of resolving them (discussed in Chapter Two).

Welfare policymaking brings into contention not only questions of fact, but also of morality, ideology and professional philosophy. How one might regard any specific reform proposal depends, among other things, on one's view of who is responsible for poverty (the individual or society), what types of intervention are efficacious (individual rehabilitation or change in the structure of income and opportunity), and how social assistance should be managed (as primarily a federal, state, local or private responsibility).

In fashioning policy, ideological beliefs in the virtues of self-sufficiency compete with sympathy for those perceived as unable to support themselves through no fault of their own. Professional beliefs in the efficacy of social work as a means of raising the poor from poverty compete with skepticism toward the value of social services and toward the poor themselves. As a brief review of welfare's history reveals, conflicting perspectives have proven remarkably immune to resolution over the past half century of policy developments.

## A Modest Beginning

Initially, the federal role in public assistance was modest and intended to remain so.[6] The Aid to Dependent Children (ADC) program established by the Social Security Act of 1935 provided only a small federal subsidy to existing state aid programs, reimbursing states for one-third of their expenses up to six dollars for the first child and four dollars for each additional child. States retained primary responsibility for determining program eligibility under the federal ADC statute, which required only that children receiving assistance be younger than 16 years old and that they be financially "deprived" because of the "death, continued absence from the house, or physical or mental incapacity of a parent."[7]

Enrollment in ADC began with about 1 million children and totalled only about 1.4 million by the end of the 1940s. In 1950, amendments to the Social Security Act extended assistance to the mothers of children qualifying for welfare and to other caretaker relatives. Following this liberalization, caseloads rose to over 2 million recipients, growing only gradually until the next expansionary surge in the 1960s.

In 1962, ADC was renamed AFDC and the federal government increased its fiscal support to between 50 and 75 percent of state welfare costs (based on a formula that takes into account state fiscal capacity). Congress also enacted several major statutory amendments in the 1960s. These amendments are illustrative of how adjustments to welfare policy have been made piecemeal and tend to incorporate, rather than resolve, divergent views of what policy should be.

For example, in the sixties, policy was liberalized to include benefits for unemployed fathers, with the proviso that they must accept jobs if made available (1961). Through grants-in-aid, federal authorities also sought to encourage rehabilitation of the poor by providing social services that would ostensibly help families climb out of poverty (1962). Later, Congress drafted both mandatory work requirements and financial work incentives—one to compel and the other to encourage able-bodied adults to participate in the labor force (1967). Mandatory work provisions required adult AFDC recipients—that is, those over age 16, out of school, and without primary responsibility for small children at home—to sign up for the WIN work incentive and training program or be cut from welfare. Work incentive provisions offered a partial disregard of earnings to welfare recipients who assumed jobs.[8]

These policy amendments also illustrated ambivalence toward the poor, a widely-recognized characteristic of American social welfare politics. As welfare caseloads changed both in size and composition, the deservingness of those on welfare was more often called into question. ADC began as a small program for orphaned children, but by 1960, it had tripled in size and

**Table 1.3**

Typical AFDC Payment to a Family of Three with No Other Income, by State:
October 1985

| | | | |
|---|---|---|---|
| Alabama | $118.00 | Montana | $332.00 |
| Alaska | 719.00 | Nebraska | 350.00 |
| Arizona | 233.00 | Nevada | 285.00 |
| Arkansas | 191.00 | New Hampshire | 389.00 |
| California | 555.00 | New Jersey | 404.00 |
| Colorado | 346.00 | New Mexico | 258.00 |
| Connecticut | 487.00 | New York | 474.00 |
| Delaware | 287.00 | North Carolina | 246.00 |
| District of Columbia | 327.00 | North Dakota | 371.00 |
| Florida | 240.00 | Ohio | 290.00 |
| Georgia | 223.00 | Oklahoma | 282.00 |
| Hawaii | 468.00 | Oregon | 397.00 |
| Idaho | 304.00 | Pennsylvania | 348.00 |
| Illinois | 302.00 | Rhode Island | 409.00 |
| Indiana | 256.00 | South Carolina | 187.00 |
| Iowa | 360.00 | South Dakota | 329.00 |
| Kansas | 365.00 | Tennessee | 153.00 |
| Kentucky | 197.00 | Texas | 184.00 |
| Louisiana | 190.00 | Utah | 376.00 |
| Maine | 370.00 | Vermont | 531.00 |
| Maryland | 329.00 | Virginia | 291.00 |
| Massachusetts | 432.00 | Washington | 462.00 |
| Michigan | 417.00 | West Virginia | 249.00 |
| Minnesota | 528.00 | Wisconsin | 544.85 |
| Mississippi | 120.00 | Wyoming | 360.00 |
| Missouri | 273.00 | | |

Source: U.S. Department of Health and Human Services, Office of Family Assistance.

only 8 percent of recipients were orphans. More doubts were raised when
67 percent of recipients qualified for aid because of the father's absence due
to imprisonment, illegitimacy, divorce or separation.

By the early 1970s, AFDC had evolved into a $5 billion national pro-
gram for which families qualified by meeting a means test and categorical
eligibility requirements. Although the federal government paid more than
half of AFDC costs, states continued to exercise primary responsibility for
welfare delivery and retained authority to set eligibility rules and payment
standards within the broad outlines of federal statutes. Then as now, states
varied in the stringency of their requirements and in the generosity of their
benefits. In 1985, typical monthly payments to a family of three ranged from
$120 in Mississippi to $555 in California. (See Table 1.3.) In general, benefits
have been set below the level of a working wage, not infrequently falling
below the official poverty line. This is consistent with the notion of maintaining welfare as an unattractive alternative to work.

### Solving One Problem, Creating Another

Even this cursory review of AFDC's development reveals something of the political struggles inherent in welfare policymaking. Questions of who the "deserving poor" are, what type of assistance they ought to receive, and how much income support should be provided have been continuously at issue as public assistance has grown from a very limited program of minimal financial support for widows and orphans to a broad program of family assistance. It is hardly surprising that Congress has tended to address these sticky questions piecemeal, without resolving moral, ideological or professional differences. As Gilbert Steiner so aptly explains, welfare programs "introduce problems of race, of sex, of religion, and of family relationships. It is hard to think of four areas most American politicians would rather avoid" (Steiner, 1966, p.4).

Of course, policy emphasis has varied over time—producing expansions of eligibility at some periods and the imposition of restrictive requirements at others.[9] Nevertheless, welfare statutes have remained, on the whole, abstract, ambiguous and internally inconsistent expressions of national policy. In effect, this has delegated difficult questions of entitlement both to the states, which have relatively broad latitude in setting eligibility and payment standards, and also to lower-level bureaucrats, who exercise discretion in applying these standards.

However, in avoiding one problem—that of settling contentious political questions of entitlement—federal and state legislators created another problem—that of controlling the distribution of welfare in a decentralized and highly-discretionary delivery system. Administrative control over welfare delivery is problematic, partly because the statutes and regulations governing its distribution are not clearly defined. The conflicting objectives embedded in welfare policy—that of helping the poor but preventing them from becoming dependent, of rehabilitating them but also policing them—have contributed to a complex welter of rules and regulations that effectively shift discretion down the policy ladder.

On the one hand, this is desirable in that it permits those closest to the scene to fit policy to individual needs and circumstances. On the other hand, it introduces problems of managerial control as lower-level workers have ample opportunity to act on their personal biases and interests. Paradoxically, as regulations are expanded to specify additional categories of eligibility and decision rules, the rules themselves become more unwieldy and difficult to understand. When welfare rules and regulations come to fill hundreds of pages (and change frequently), there is even greater likelihood that workers will exercise their own judgment or use their discretion to find shortcuts in making decisions about benefits.

Every determination or redetermination of eligibility may require workers to verify between 25 and 40 aspects of eligibility—such as residence, age, family relationships, ineligibility for other types of assistance, earnings, school attendance, work registration, and work experience. In many states, case workers conduct home visits as well as in-office interviews with grantees. Not only do policies change frequently, but also they may require detailed calculations (for example, of average monthly earnings after allowable deductions) and difficult decisions (for example, how to allocate child care expenses when custody is shared). These activities must be carried out in the midst of special administrative projects, routine case maintenance, requests for referrals and emergency assistance, and other tasks, accompanied by voluminous paperwork requirements. All too commonly, the institutional resources available to help caseworkers are limited, and caseloads are large. (It is not unusual for a single worker to be responsible for 100 to 200 cases.)

Before welfare caseloads exploded in the latter part of the sixties, the political advantages of delegating difficult questions of entitlement down the policy chain may have outweighed the disadvantages in lost accountability. However, these disadvantages assumed new and critical importance as state caseloads and, hence, federal payments to states, began to soar. The federal government lacked direct control over expenditures for welfare and other entitlements that were based strictly on demand. Financially, the federal government was vulnerable to states that, through indifference or intent, opened the floodgates to demands for welfare. In these circumstances, relying on state discretion to manage the distribution of welfare was far less attractive.[10]

Comprehensive legislative reform might have simplified the delivery of welfare and reduced state discretion by setting clear, federal eligibility and payment standards. But, in lieu of that, how was the federal government to assert managerial control over nominally autonomous state welfare bureaucracies? How could responsiveness to national authorities and concern for controlling costs be transmitted through a multi-layered welfare system staffed, largely, by lower-level workers vested with considerable discretion? These were among the problems that administrative reform sought to address.

## The Promise of Reform: Some Unanswered Questions

Administrative reform promised to clean up the mess in welfare by improving state performance in the delivery of public assistance. Reform had broad appeal as a means of protecting the poor from arbitrary bureaucratic practices, protecting the taxpayer from waste and misuse of public funds, and even protecting social welfare programs from disrepute engendered by charges of fraud, waste and abuse.

The chief mechanism of administrative reform was quality control, a performance monitoring system that assessed the accuracy of state welfare payments. Federal authorities used this mechanism to reach out to the states that delivered welfare benefits and hold them fiscally responsible for their payment practices. Without directly infringing on the autonomy of state

**Table 1.4**

AFDC Quality Control Error Rates* for Massachusetts
and the Nation: 1973–1982†

|  | 4/73– 9/73 | 1/74– 6/74 | 7/74– 12/74 | 1/75– 6/75 | 7/75– 12/75 | 1/76– 6/76 | 7/76– 12/76 | 1/77– 6/77 |
|---|---|---|---|---|---|---|---|---|
| National Average | 16.5 | 14.8‡ | 13.6‡ | 12.0‡ | 11.2 | 9.6 | 8.5 | 8.6 |
| Massachusetts | 15.9 | 17.1‡ | 17.9‡ | 19.8‡ | 14.8 | 13.1 | 12.0 | 12.8 |

|  | 7/77– 12/77 | 1/78– 6/78 | 4/78– 9/78 | 10/78– 3/79 | 4/79– 9/79 | 10/79– 3/80 | 4/80– 9/80 | 10/80– 3/81 | 4/81– 9/82 |
|---|---|---|---|---|---|---|---|---|---|
| National Average | 8.7 | 9.5 | 9.4 | 10.4 | 9.5 | 8.3 | 7.3 | 8.3 | 7.0 |
| Massachusetts | 11.6 | 15.9 | 15.9 | 24.8 | 22.4 | 16.7 | 8.2 | 11.1 | 7.4 |

Sources: U.S. Dept. of Health, Education and Welfare; Massachusetts Department of Public Welfare.
* Federal estimates of overpayments and payments to ineligible persons as a percentage of total payments, except where noted by double dagger (‡) as a non-regression formula estimate.
† Includes newly defined payment errors involving compliance with social security enumeration and child support requirements after 1978.

welfare administration, the federal government indirectly encouraged reform by imposing fiscal penalties on states for erroneous welfare payments.[11] Significantly, federal penalties applied only to overpayments and payments to ineligible individuals. States were not held accountable for or encouraged to reform poor management practices that resulted in underpayments and erroneous denials of assistance. First applied to the AFDC program in 1973, quality control monitoring and fiscal sanctions eventually were extended to the other major social welfare programs, including food stamps, Medicaid and supplemental security income. (Provisions vary for each program.)

After more than a decade of administrative reform, what do we know about it? For the most part, what we know is based on analyses of the management problems encountered in welfare and the technical initiatives taken to resolve them.[12] The most significant of these initiatives occurred in response to the federal government's threat to impose fiscal sanctions against states that had high rates of payment errors. (The error rate is a measure of the percentage of benefits incorrectly paid out.) Looking at data on errors, it would appear that administrative reform was remarkably successful. Nationally, AFDC payment error rates declined from about 16.5 percent in 1973 to 7 percent by 1981. (See Table 1.4.)

From a strictly managerial perspective, then, administrative reform appeared to have worked rather well. But it certainly runs contrary to conventional wisdom to imagine that a decentralized and, in many respects, inchoate federal bureaucracy could provide an avenue for redirecting welfare policy. The more prevalent view, to paraphrase Pressman and Wildavsky (1973), is to wonder why anything works at all. It is far more common to regard public bureaucracies as a source of stability or even inertia rather than as an instrument of change. Bureaucracies are typically depicted as quasi-autonomous political actors operating in behalf of their own perceived interests. Policy produced through bureaucratic mechanisms is rife with "unanticipated consequences."[13]

However, bureaucracies are more than policy deliverers or semi-independent policy actors. They are also institutions that give definition and structure to policy politics. First, it may be virtually unarguable that the welfare system should help those entitled to assistance and keep others out. However, in practice, it is often unclear who is entitled to welfare and how one determines eligibility. Commonsensical terms such as "fairness" ignore the allocative question of how much of the burden of determining eligibility should be placed on applicants by requiring that they prove their entitlement and how much on the system by requiring that it prove claims of need are false. Should the passageway to welfare be fully opened, halfway opened, or mostly closed? These choices are distinctly political in that they have distributive consequences. The policy effects of these choices may occur at the margins, but in a system recognized for its incrementalism, marginal shifts are significant. Second, in a more diffuse and symbolic sense, choices about the terms on which welfare will be distributed express differing visions of the welfare state—one more limited and begrudging, another more expansive and embracing.

Graham Allison (1971) has taught a generation of public policy analysts that "what you see depends on where you sit." If one applies a political lens to an examination of administrative welfare reform, what does one see? What vision of welfare did it express? Did its outcomes extend beyond simply removing the undeserving from the welfare rolls? What was reform's relationship to policy politics, that is, the politics of what welfare should be? These questions form the core of this inquiry.

## The Origins and Scope of This Inquiry

My initial glimpse into the potential political significance of administrative welfare reform came from discussions with legal services attorneys in Boston. Massachusetts had pursued administrative reform with great vigor and, by all indications, had achieved remarkable success. The state's reform drive began in 1979 and in only two years had driven down payment errors by nearly 67 percent. The state's error rate dropped from 24.8 percent (the second highest in the nation after Alaska) to 8.2 percent, and officials proudly claimed that they had substantially cleaned up the welfare mess in Massachusetts. (See Table 1.4.)

But if the welfare system had suddenly become 67 percent more accurate and its bureaucracy more uniform and conscientious in its treatment of clients, it was hard to tell that from the cases that were pouring into legal services offices across the state. Increasing reports from clients of harassment, indifference, and procedural obstacles to welfare were strongly at odds with the state's reform claims and its manifest success.

In deciding to investigate administrative reform in Massachusetts, I sought an explanation for these different portrayals of the reformed bureaucracy. Had administrative reform improved welfare delivery, making the bureaucracy fairer and more efficient as state officials claimed? Or had reform been translated into procedural barriers to assistance that systematically limited the availability of benefits to poor families ostensibly entitled to receive them?

If reform had improved welfare delivery—that is, insured that those entitled to aid received it and the undeserving did not—then Massachusetts would illustrate "how to do it," a much needed example of competence in government. But what if, instead, reform had resulted in procedural restrictions that effectively imparted a new and more limited meaning to welfare as an entitlement? In that case, Massachusetts could provide insights into a virtually invisible form of policymaking that might function as an alternative to political mechanisms for redefining social policy.

This book is an outgrowth and elaboration of that inquiry. It presents a detailed analysis of the reform process, describing its origins at the national level and its influence on decentralized and nominally autonomous state and street-level bureaucracies. This case study of administrative welfare reform is set within a political framework that draws attention to the institutional importance of alternative mechanisms for expressing, channeling, and mediating political conflict over the parameters of the American welfare state.

## Notes on Methodology and Organization

The primary evidence for this analysis of administrative welfare reform is drawn from the Massachusetts case. Because of its exceptional intensity and dramatic results, the Massachusetts case offered an opportunity to gain insights into processes and effects that would be even more difficult to discern if more gradual and modest. However, administrative welfare reform was not confined to Massachusetts but was pursued by most other large states experiencing mushrooming welfare caseloads in the late sixties and early seventies. Analyses of their experiences (reviewed in Chapter Seven) lend support to the claim that the reform effort in Massachusetts, while it may have been more intense than most (and thus easier to observe), was not unique.

Nor is administrative reform unique to AFDC. As noted earlier, similar administrative techniques and reforms have been used in other major entitlement programs. Moreover, administrative initiatives, similar to those described in this book, have been expanded and intensified in conjunction with the Reagan Administration's efforts to reduce social spending.

However, this analysis is rooted, not in the overt cutback politics of the Reagan Administration, but in the seventies, a period of cross-cutting currents in the policy politics of welfare. It is in the specific context of concern over rising welfare rolls and stalemated legislative reform that I examine administrative reform as an alternative means of restricting welfare.

Although this study has broad relevance, it is a single case and, like any other, is limited by its particularities. Generalizations must be regarded as more suggestive than definitive. However, an advantage of the in-depth case study rooted in a specific context is that it may illuminate aspects of process and politics that one might miss altogether or mistake from a broader, but more distant, vantage point. To quote Hugh Heclo: "We deal in that difficult but perhaps rewarding middle zone—between the large questions with no determinate answers and the small questions of tiresome and often insignificant conclusiveness. As usual, the challenge is to find a balance between being irrefutable and being worth refuting" (1974, p. 16).

Most of the data for this study were collected between 1980 and 1982, from interviews, direct observation, and a review of official and unofficial documents made available to me by several congressional committees; the U.S. Department of Health and Human Services (HHS), formerly the Department of Health, Education and Welfare (HEW); the Massachusetts Department of Public Welfare (MDPW); and secondary sources. In the course of this research, I conducted extensive, formal interviews with more than 75 state and federal officials, congressional aides, lobbyists, attorneys, welfare activists, and welfare workers.[14] Other, less formal discussions occurred in the course of direct observation in local welfare offices, at meetings of state and local welfare advisory boards, and at meetings of the state Welfare Coalition (an organization of legal services lawyers and poor people's advocates). My observations of the welfare eligibility determination process and quality control and quality assurance reviews were made in Boston welfare offices between January 1981 and May 1982. I obtained access and insights into the client side of these processes as a resident policy analyst at the Legal Services Institute in Boston. The Institute provided legal services to the poor and clinical training to law students.

With few exceptions, I do not attribute information I received in interviews to specific individuals, as I promised anonymity to those who spoke with me. In some cases, those interviewed might have jeopardized their positions by their candid remarks. Also, any specific cases cited in the text have been altered slightly and names changed in order to protect the privacy of welfare recipients and legal services clients. I have tried to make no alterations that would distort the meaning of the information used.

This book is organized into seven chapters, the next of which sets out a theoretical framework for the analysis of administrative welfare reform. Chapters Three and Four discuss how administrative reform emerged from the welfare politics of the seventies and came to embody a particular vision of what welfare should be. Chapters Five and Six describe the Massachusetts response to federal reform pressures and how state managerial initiatives began to redefine welfare policy. Chapter Six focuses on the responses of bureaucrats at the street level to the organizational environment created by administrative reform and how those responses "added up" to restrictions on the distribution of welfare. Chapter Seven draws on case material to elaborate the theoretical premises that guided this inquiry. It discusses the implications of my findings for social welfare policymaking, practice, and politics.

# 2

# An Alternative to Policy Politics

Alternatives to legislative means of policymaking would be unnecessary if the American political system functioned as our ideals would have it. According to a simplistic model of democratic policymaking, voters elect representatives who they believe will express their policy preferences. The legislation that emerges from policy debate is then implemented by an apolitical bureaucracy of experts. Almost no one would assert that is how democracies work in practice.

## Theories of Political Deadlock

A more complicated pluralist model generally depicts policymaking as a product of bargaining and compromise within the legislature and among legislators, the President, bureaucrats, and interest groups, with the courts running interference for aggrieved interests. From this perspective, it is common to conclude that, although messy, the policymaking system works reasonably well, change is incremental, and we muddle through.[1]

However, some analysts in the pluralist tradition have come to regard interest-group liberalism as not so much the integument of the policymaking process but as a source of policy disarray, confusion, and stalemate. So-called "governability crisis theory" seeks to explain "ungovernability" in terms of what Samuel P. Huntington describes as weaknesses in both the "inputting" and "outputting" functions of the state and in the institutional bridges that link these two functions.[2] The broad outlines of this argument, as they relate to the problem of authoritative policymaking, can be crudely summarized as follows. Political parties that traditionally provided the institutional means of articulating and aggregating interests have been in decline, accompanied by large-scale political disorganization and demobilization. Elections, as a means of linking citizens to the state, cannot be said to perform that function when a growing proportion of citizens do not vote or when their votes are disassociated from meaningful clusters of policy issues.

The disorganization in the inputting institutions of governance is reflected in the diminished capacity of outputting institutions. Congress is internally fragmented, not only structurally but also politically. Its members (especially those in the House) are oriented toward parochial interests and, increasingly, toward the constituency service functions that assure them reelection. They have insufficient incentives and capacity to resolve political conflict over policy in such a way as to establish coherent and responsive national policies. Walter Dean Burnham describes this phenomenon in terms of the withering of

> traditional partisan channels connecting the rulers and the ruled, across the great fault lines at the center known as "separation of powers.".
> . . . [The] fragmented pluralism this constitutional structure encourages keeps growing. Political executives, legislators, and judges have every incentive to go into business for themselves and for their clients; and they do. (Burnham, 1980, p. 149)

If Congress cannot resolve policy conflicts and manage the affairs of state, neither can the President. According to Huntington, James Sundquist, and Anthony King, among others, the President is the only institutional figure representing a national constituency and potentially in a position to formulate timely and coherent policy responses to national problems. However, presidential authority is limited by the separation of powers. And, as the party system decays, linkages between the "party-in-the-electorate," the "party-in-Congress," and the "party-in-the-White House" also erode. The consequence is that presidential efforts to direct national affairs become bogged down in institutional stalemate.

These weaknesses in the interest-aggregating, conflict-solving, and policymaking institutions of governance assume critical proportion as the responsibilities of the state increase and the demands of its citizens multiply and intensify. Anthony King refers to this as the "democratic overload," reflecting both the extension of the state into spheres that were formerly left to individuals and the marketplace and the inadequate restraints on the opportunities for citizens to make demands on the state. According to Huntington's analysis, this produces a crisis of authority resulting from

> a substantial increase in governmental activity and a substantial decrease in governmental authority. . . . Paradoxically, . . . this working out of the democratic impulse was associated with the shift in the relative balance in the political system between the decline of the more political, interest-aggregating, "input" institutions of government (most notably, political parties and the presidency), on the one hand, and

the growth in the bureaucratic, regulating and implementing, "output" institutions of government, on the other. (Huntington, 1975, p. 64)

The political stalemate over comprehensive reform reached in the wake of the welfare crisis closely resembled that type of disorganized policy paralysis predicted by governability theory.

Furthermore, its corollary, the disorganized mess in welfare management, might have been predicted as well. Sundquist writes of a "crisis of competence" in the bureaucratic "outputting" side of government. He argues that the business of the state is poorly run, with its executive constrained in taking authoritative action and its policy delivery apparatus left in the hands of "amateurs." As Sundquist avers: "No business organization operates that way or could survive if it did" (Sundquist, 1980, p. 203).[3]

The inability of the state to resolve political conflict through "normal" institutional channels is explained by neo-Marxist theory in terms of the contradictions of democratic capitalism and weaknesses in the democratic institutions that link the citizen to the state. The essential contradiction of democratic capitalism, according to James O'Connor, Piven and Cloward, and Ira Katznelson, among others,[4] derives from the state's need to protect the accumulation of capital while responding to democratic demands for equality, redistribution, and social welfare protections. Democratic support is necessary for governance, but so is the generation of surplus value that sustains the economy.

As the state role in providing for social welfare and protecting capitalist accumulation becomes both more intrusive and more transparent, the state's actions become politicized and difficult to legitimate. If, simultaneously, there is a weakening in the institutions that link the citizen to the state, then a crisis of legitimacy will ensue. As Claus Offe (1979, p. 21) explains, a legitimation crisis will occur when "the institutional link between the individual and the state has been attenuated [but] the actual links between the state and the individual become ever more direct." This tension is exacerbated during periods of fiscal strain, when state economic management raises difficult, zero-sum choices. This was the context within which the welfare crisis emerged in the early seventies.

## An Alternative to Political Deadlock: Managing Policy Politics

Oddly, both pluralist and neo-Marxist theories appear headed toward conclusions of political deadlock, although arriving there by different analytic routes.[5] But that is not where the road ends. Claus Offe has hypothesized that when political forms of conflict articulation and resolution deteriorate and democratic linkages between citizen and state become attenuated, "alternative political forms both of the articulation of conflict and the resolution of policy issues appear" (Offe, 1984, p. 21). How that might work or the specific attributes of such alternative forms are suggested but not fully spelled out. The remainder of this chapter sets out a conceptual framework for examining administrative welfare reform as a means of making manageable the unruly politics of welfare policy. It considers the resources, mechanisms, and possible effects one should look for in the course of such an examination.

Bureaucratic discretion, an important political resource for administrative agencies, is a feature of the administrative state that deservedly has received a great deal of analytical attention. In a sense, the New Deal model of administration raised bureaucratic discretion to a virtue, favoring the rationalization of policy decisions on the basis of expertise. Moreover, expertise was to be insulated from central political control, as reflected in the popularity of independent regulatory commissions during the New Deal.[6] One ironic consequence of the decentralization of functional expertise among administrative agencies and commissions was that, in protecting them from central political control, it made them susceptible to capture by specialized clientele groups.

Another form of administrative discretion is that which occurs when agencies participate in interest-group politics. Agencies participate in bargaining over policy as advocates of a particular constituency or in behalf of bureaucratic interests, such as power, fiscal resources, autonomy, and so forth. Administrative discretion exercised in this context is part of what Emmette Redford refers to as "subsystem or intermediary politics . . . involving the interrelations of bureaus and other administrative operating agencies, the counterpart congressional committee structure, and the interest organizations, trade press, and lobbyists concerned with a particular area of program specialization" (Redford, 1969, p. 83). So pervasive is the bureaucracy's role as a quasi-independent political actor that, according to Theodore Lowi, it has been incorporated within the justifying ideology of "interest-group liberalism" (Lowi, 1979).

However, bureaucratic discretion is not limited to matters calling for the provision of expert advice nor to interest-group bargaining. It has a more direct application when the agencies that implement policy, in practice, make policy by giving it operational meaning. In part, this is a logical necessity, given the complexity of the tasks that government undertakes through its bureaucracy. But, in part, it is the result of political conditions that, effectively, have vested greater policy authority in the bureaucracy.

Policy complexity provides a partial explanation for the wide range of bureaucratic discretion. It would be impossible to delineate policy legislatively in such detail that bureaucratic discretion could be eliminated. Nor might that be desirable with respect to flexibility and adaptiveness. There is an inherent tradeoff between specificity and rigidity and also between specificity and unwieldiness.[7] For many federal programs, the rules are already so voluminous that their managers become bogged down in paperwork. Or, administrative criteria may be so detailed and complex that they are virtually inaccessible to those who must apply them.

It is reasonably straightforward to justify bureaucratic discretion that has the manifest purpose of avoiding rigidity and unwieldiness. However, there is another source of bureaucratic discretion that requires political explanation. It derives from the tacit delegation of policymaking authority by Congress, referred to by Lowi. He blames it, in part, on "typical American politicians [who] displace and defer and delegate conflict where possible; they face conflict squarely only when they must." But they prefer to delegate "as far down the line as possible" (Lowi, 1979, p. 55). This propensity is expressed in the enactment of vague and ambiguous legislation that, according to Lowi, appears more the product of logrolling and compromise than of authoritative decisionmaking.

### How Operations Become Policy

Another source of discretion derives from the relative autonomy with which public bureaucrats operate under certain circumstances. This is well documented in the case of "street-level bureaucrats" who deliver services.[8] In the field, they find many opportunities to exercise "unauthorized discretion"; that is, they may behave in ways that, intentionally or unintentionally, subvert policy objectives, even loosely defined ones. When bureaucratic interests—in a simpler work routine, in greater power over their clients, or in personal autonomy—conflict with those of management, they have the resources to act in their own behalf rather than as agents of their organizations.

According to Michael Lipsky's theory of street-level bureaucracy, under certain conditions policy actually is made from the bottom up. He asserts that policy is most likely to be made by those closest to the point of delivery when their jobs involve a relatively great degree of discretion, when they must choose among multiple objectives and tasks, and when policy implementation involves changes in established practice (Lipsky, 1978). Street-level bureaucrats' discretion in operationalizing policy gives them considerable, but disaggregated, influence over the shape and substance of policy-as-delivered.

Operational decisions come in many shapes and vary in importance. They may occur through formal processes (for example, regulation) or informal ones (for example, decision rules) and may originate at the top of the bureaucratic hierarchy or at the bottom. In addition, regardless of their form and origin, they may be either systematic or unsystematic in their policy effects. It is only when they are systematic that we can speak of bureaucratic or informal policymaking. Formal policymaking is subject to procedural safeguards that protect against bureaucratic abuses of discretion and, to a greater or lesser degree, invite public participation and scrutiny. In contrast, informal policymaking operates outside the reach of most safeguards and most citizens,[9] a point to which I will return later.

Systematic, informal policymaking often occurs in the form of a production problem. For example, Philippe Nonet describes how the Industrial Accident Commission (IAC) responded to increased claims for worker compensation by shortcutting its quasi-judicial deliberative procedures. Employing the rationale that "justice delayed is justice denied," the IAC used a variety of informal tactics to "dissuade, if not prevent . . . parties from asserting their rights" in commission proceedings. Commission members curbed the use of continuances, discouraged cross-examination of experts, and informally pressured claimants to settle privately (which usually meant for less compensation) (Nonet, 1969, esp. ch. 2).

Ironically, mechanisms manifestly intended to improve policy delivery by improving productivity may have the most adverse systematic policy effects. For example, Occupational Safety and Health Administration (OSHA) inspectors must meet productivity requirements that specify a certain number of factory inspections per month. It is a reasonable requirement aimed at insuring that workers are protected from exposure to contaminants, as the law provides. But what if, under pressure of productivity requirements, an OSHA inspector takes shortcuts on inspection visits, failing to follow up suspect but not overtly impermissible factory practices or shortening testing time for monitoring air quality so that contamination cannot be detected? Now, what if cuts in OSHA's budget have been distributed so as to drastically reduce the number of inspectors? One might well assume that if productivity pressures intensify across the board, shortcuts will become common practice among the beleaguered inspectors. Although the coping responses of these street-level bureaucrats occur individually, in the aggregate they would follow a consistent pattern and produce systematic policy effects.[10]

The most important lesson to draw from these examples is that apparently unsystematic and uncoordinated bureaucratic behaviors, manifestly neutral administrative processes, or minor changes in administrative routine may produce systematic policy effects. As Charles Lindblom acknowledged in modifying his theory of incrementalism, even small-scale, incremental policy changes may produce substantive and non-incremental policy effects (Lindblom, 1979).

Of course, bureaucratic discretion is not unconstrained. Formal, or statutory, policymaking sets the boundaries within which informal, bureaucratic, policymaking occurs (Rein and Rabinovitz, 1978). However, these boundary areas are blurred when legislation is vague and broadly worded and when legislators, effectively, delegate choices to the agencies that implement policy. In this context, the actions that administrative agencies take to operationalize policy are imbued with political significance because they embody policy choices.

## Administration and the Scope of Conflict

But how is discretion a resource for managing policy conflict? When politics is described as unmanageable, it indicates, among other things, that conflicts are broad in scope and institutional processes for settling them are inadequate. Put bluntly, there are too many difficult issues, too many active participants, and too few opportunities for authoritative resolution and action. If administrative agencies were to manage policy politics, then they ought to be able to reduce the volume and difficulty of issues, limit participation, and provide an alternative to political forms of conflict resolution. Based on the prior discussion, it is possible to offer some propositions that suggest how administrative agencies may perform these functions, more or less effectively.

Administrative agencies may limit participation in policymaking, in part, by transforming policymaking into a series of apparently uncoordinated, diffuse operational activities. As the preceding examples indicate, policymaking that occurs as a by-product of bureaucratic routine, lower-level coping mechanisms, and informal decision rules is difficult to identify analytically, much less challenge politically. This, of course, is a virtue in terms of managing political conflict over policy. Informal bureaucratic policymaking circumvents the pitfalls of more explicit, formal policymaking precisely because it is incremental and obscured. Administrative agencies also reduce the volume and intractability of issues by transforming them into non-issues. For example, they tend to avoid making explicitly allocative decisions but nevertheless distribute government benefits and services as a consequence of operational decisions that are manifestly nonpolitical. At times, administrative agencies may work in tandem with politicians who try to depoliticize policy choices by reframing them to appeal to widely shared values, say, efficiency or science.

In addition, policymaking that occurs in the administrative arena may be participation-limiting because, when conflict is transferred to that arena, it is also transformed and the salient issues redefined as administrative, technical, or scientific. On this point, Offe asserts that "as soon as an issue is institutionally defined as requiring scientific advice and expertise, the scope of legitimate participants is drastically reduced" (1979, p. 9). Even those who argue that "participation [is] good for the soul of the citizen . . . [and] necessary for the viability of democracy" have difficulty reconciling this view with the technical intricacies involved in resolving "technically intensive public policy disputes." Writing on this issue, Harvey Brooks concludes that "it is unrealistic and impractical to appeal every issue— especially complex, technically oriented issues—to a public process. To be meaningful, public participation must be conducted on a highly selective basis, thereby promoting experts as the principal actors in most public policy decisions involving technical information" (Brooks, 1984, p. 49).[11]

Finally, if administrative agencies provide an alternative to political forms of policy resolution, it is not only because they can make policy without seeming to, but also because they can legitimate their actions by representing them to be nonpolitical. One would expect the greatest degree of nonpolitical legitimation to be required for those administrative activities that are most visibly policy-relevant, such as regulation. The array of technical trappings within which environmental regulations are made (cost-benefit analysis, risk assessment, and so forth) may be necessary to provide nonpolitical justification for allocative decisions as well as to provide information to decisionmakers.[12]

To summarize, administrative activities may be undertaken in the name of a manifestly nonpolitical purpose. Moreover, they may appear to be ad hoc and initiated at the lower reaches of the bureaucracy. However, these activities may produce systematic policy consequences, which in the aggregate become policy. A latent function[13] of this process is to make policy politics more manageable by: (1) de-politicizing policy choices, (2) limiting participation in the policymaking process, (3) making policy without appearing to, and (4) legitimating administrative practices on the basis of widely held, nonpolitical values.

This is not to suggest that some cynical conspiracy underlies all administrative activity. Quite the contrary, administrative agencies may manage policy politics even when bureaucrats within them are both manifestly and actually working toward the nonpolitical purpose they purport to be or even when their behaviors would appear to be, in the aggregate, nonpurposeful. An example of the latter would be the standard operating procedures that emerge as a by-product of coping mechanisms street-level bureaucrats develop to deal with multiple demands. Even these behaviors, viewed at a broader level, may have systematic effects that serve a latent, political function. Take the case of welfare workers who cope with burdensome caseloads by treating clients perfunctorily or even rudely. The effect of such behaviors, as Jeffrey Prottas (1981) has shown, may be to discourage requests for help and thus effectively "ration" access to ostensibly available social entitlements.

### Strategic Use of the Bureaucracy

The management of policy politics may occur in both structured and unstructured forms—the latter presenting the more difficult empirical problem. However, precisely because it is less visible, it may be the more effective.

At times, public officials consciously and systematically use nonpolitical means to pursue political objectives. Activities that have occurred under the rubric of the "administrative presidency" are a case in point. An objective of Nixon's administrative presidency strategy that Richard Nathan has described was to gain control of bureaucratic policymaking processes in order to achieve policy objectives, some of which had been blocked when presented as part of the Administration's legislative program. In important respects, the administrative presidency strategy underscores the strategic, political value of administrative agencies. Nathan writes:

> Nixon came to the conclusion some time in 1971 that in many areas of government, particularly domestic affairs, *operations is policy*. Many day-to-day management tasks for domestic programs—for example, regulation writing, grant approval, and budget apportionment—are substantive and therefore involve policy. The White House counter-bureaucracy could not penetrate deeply enough into the operations of government on any kind of systematic basis to effect these essentially managerial processes. Gaining greater control over agency policy setting and managerial processes was the aim of Nixon's administrative presidency strategy in his second term. (Nathan, 1983, pp. 45–47)

In effect, the administrative presidency strategy aimed to use administrative agencies intentionally to manage policy politics and to direct this process from the White House. In this case, the "benefits" of managing policy politics were not, primarily, diffuse or system-functional; rather they accrued to the Executive. Among the strategy's benefits were that the Administration could direct policy from within the bureaucracies that delivered it, avoiding legislative scrutiny and obscuring the thrust of presidential policy initiatives.

Administrative welfare reform was initially part of that intentional strategy to manipulate policy through bureaucratic means. But it became much more than that. Reform had greater persistence than its originators. Once initiated, it assumed the aura of an idea whose time had come. Reform became, in certain aspects, part of policy politics, a medium through which both liberals and conservatives sought to define welfare policy. It also began to penetrate the operational routines of the decentralized state and local-level bureaucracies that delivered welfare and, ultimately, determined its distribution.

# 3

## Origins and Evolution of Administrative Reform

As an issue, administrative reform was manifestly nonpolitical. But issues do not arise independent of political context. It is only in context that one can understand why certain "conditions" become "issues" and how those "issues" come to define the boundaries of policy politics.[1] With the emergence of the welfare crisis in the seventies, there began a transition from a prevailing concern with poverty's causes and cures to an overriding concern with welfare's costs and mismanagement. This redefinition of the welfare "problem" was associated with a subtle shift in the locus of policy politics from the legislative to the administrative arena. Such shifts are important strategically because the arena and terms of policy conflicts have bearing on their scope and, ultimately, their outcomes.[2]

### Defining the Issues

Welfare's rapid growth at the end of the sixties created a new point of departure for conflict over welfare policy. The central issue was the welfare "mess," an evocative, but not very meaningful, term. Did it mean that confusing policy and chaotic administration were impeding the translation of "new property rights"[3] into reality? Did it mean that rampant fraud, waste, and abuse were going unchecked? Did it signify that welfare was too generous and implicitly encouraging dependency, or that it was too stingy and failing to provide adequate relief? Defining the welfare mess was more a political than an analytical problem. The emerging definition of the welfare crisis, although framed in consensual nonpolitical terms, came to embrace certain political beliefs about welfare and exclude others.[4]

#### The "Official" Crisis

The welfare system was officially declared to be in "crisis" in the seventies. In 1972, the Subcommittee on Fiscal Policy of Congress's Joint

Economic Committee reported a "crisis in public welfare" that "has deepened over the years" (U.S. Congress, Joint Economic Committee, 1972b, p. v). The subcommittee expressed concern that the rapid growth in AFDC caseloads had overwhelmed state administrative systems, which lacked the capacity to manage a program grown so large and complex. In its report, the subcommittee characterized the welfare delivery system as "an administrative nightmare," in which "confusion, inefficiency, and lawlessness" were pervasive (U.S. Congress, Joint Economic Committee, 1972b, p. vi). Furthermore, the report stated that "many of the problems... have grown out of certain administrative practices which may have outlived their usefulness in the face of changes in clientele, in administrative personnel and workloads, and in public expectations about program management and integrity" (U.S. Congress, Joint Economic Committee, 1972b, p. v).

The subcommittee viewed the crisis as rooted in statutory complexities, which made welfare "impossible" to administer. However, this was only one interpretation of the crisis. Other interpretations and proposals for comprehensive statutory reform reflected fundamentally different points of view on the appropriate scope of the state's social welfare role and on the deservingness of the poor themselves. These conflicts are threaded throughout the history of American welfare politics.

## "Malingerers," "Cheats," and "Frauds"

In the aftermath of the welfare explosion, doubts about the "deservingness" of those seeking assistance were expressed in a rising chorus of attacks on welfare "cheats." A key figure in this attack was Russell B. Long, chairman of the Senate Finance Committee. He contended that AFDC had "mushroomed without planning, grown like Topsy, until it... caused the entire program to take on the appellation of the 'welfare mess'" (U.S. Congress, Senate, 1972, p. 3). Moreover, he argued that sloppy state welfare practices had permitted cheating, fraud, and abuse to swell the welfare rolls.

In an address on welfare cheating to the Senate, he stated:

> The rhetorical question proposed by the passage from the Bible—"Am I my brother's keeper?"—should be answered with a resounding "Yes," but only when we refer to the destitute, the disabled, and the orphaned. . . . But I am concerned—gravely concerned—that the welfare system, as we know it today, is being manipulated and abused by malingerers, cheats and outright frauds to the detriment not only of the American taxpayers whose dollars support the program, but also to the detriment of the truly needy on whose behalf the Federal-State system of cash assistance is so important.[5]

He contended that stricter administrative procedures and tighter rules were necessary to protect the welfare system and, ultimately, the poor themselves. However, Long's critique of the welfare system went beyond administrative sloppiness to identify unspecified numbers of recipients (the "cheats and frauds") as the chief cause of the welfare mess.

## The Administrative Nightmare

Liberal social welfare advocates readily agreed that state welfare administration was a "mess." But, in contrast to Long, they criticized the administrative nightmare for preventing poor families from obtaining their social entitlements and were less concerned that "cheats" might be penetrating the system. From the liberal perspective, growing welfare rolls were evidence, not of disaster, but of reform—an indication that previously unaided poor families were beginning to receive assistance (Holmer, 1975). This reform was a product of two key forces. The first was a political mobilization by groups of organized recipients in response to which administrators had eliminated some of the institutional barriers and oppressive administrative practices (such as home searches) that had discouraged welfare applicants (Bailis, 1974). The second was a "legalization strategy" that had successfully extended legal protection to welfare claims (Rosenblatt, 1982).

Full realization of welfare rights was the goal of liberal reformers, who recognized that, in welfare as in other programs, the delivery of social entitlements depends on administrative action. Thus, in programs such as welfare that are implemented through a decentralized system within which lower-level bureaucrats exercise considerable discretion, delivery is far from guaranteed.

Writing in 1968, HEW Secretary Wilbur Cohen expressed both the hopes and concerns of liberal reformers, asserting that:

> Today there is a growing recognition of the legal right to the receipt of public assistance, a legal right to invoke the Constitution to assure the fairness of the system. What lies ahead is the task of applying these rights, point by point, so that the poor may come to stand truly equal before the law. (Cohen, quoted in Steiner, 1971, p. 90)

From the perspective of at least one legal scholar, it seemed that the implementation problem was central to the "administrative mess" in welfare and, furthermore, constituted a denial of due process and a continuing impediment to the realization of welfare rights. In order to bridge the gap between the law's guarantees of a social entitlement and state implementation of welfare statutes, Jerome Mashaw proposed using quality control to enforce greater state procedural regularity. According to Mashaw, the virtue of this mechanism was its adaptability. He commented that "a quality control system can be adapted to virtually any type of enterprise or end product for it involves merely the development of standards, the evaluation of performance against these standards, and the action to upgrade substandard performance" (Mashaw, 1974, p. 791).

Such an approach was "straightforward and sensible" and grounded in definitions of "fairness" and "accuracy" on which agreement could be reached. Mashaw, using a legalistic interpretation of these terms, proposed that "fairness is . . . promoted by presumptions which skew the cases in the direction of positive determinants which, therefore, reallocate the burden of proof so that lack of technical or financial resources will not bar some otherwise valid claims" (Mashaw, 1974, p. 791). "Substantive accuracy," in contrast to procedural uniformity, required that quality control measure agency decisions with regard to the "facts."[6] What Mashaw failed to confront was that his definitions did not spring from either legal necessity or "objective" administrative logic, although both could be used to justify those definitions. Rather, definitions of administrative criteria, such as those Mashaw proposed, represented a political preference, one that gave greater weight to making welfare accessible than to restricting it.

### Uncontrollable Costs

In the seventies, the concerns of those who believed that the chaos in state welfare administration effectively abridged entitlement rights were transcended by what Lester Salamon has described as a "widespread concern that welfare spending has gone out of control and that drastic corrective action is necessary" (Salamon, 1978, p. 17). Amid growing fears of continued increases in welfare rolls and "uncontrollable" spending, the cost issue became, as Salamon put it, "the fulcrum" on which welfare policy turned (Salamon, 1978, p. 17). It is in this context that a new wave of reform demands emerged. But they faced what Martin Anderson has described as the "reform dilemma." That is:

> To become a political reality the [reform] plan must provide a decent level of support for those on welfare, it must contain strong incentives to work, and it must have a reasonable cost. And it must do all three at the same time. If any one of these parts is missing or deficient, the reform plan is nakedly vulnerable to anyone who wishes to attack and condemn it. (Anderson, 1978, p. 135)

By that reasoning, one could well argue that any reform plan would be "nakedly vulnerable" because there is unlikely to be agreement on what is a decent level of support, how to provide assistance without undermining the work ethic, or, for that matter, angering the working poor not receiving welfare. "Reasonableness" is in the eye of the beholder. In the case of welfare costs, it depends heavily on one's philosophical perspective regarding the proper role of the state in providing social assistance and on the perceived distribution of costs as well as benefits.

In its first term, the Nixon Administration sought to deal with this dilemma by fashioning a comprehensive legislative reform package that more or less incorporated very disparate views of the welfare crisis and what welfare should be. The Family Assistance Plan (FAP) reflected, among other things, the Administration's need to build a coalition among diverse interests. Indeed, FAP appeared to have something for everyone. It offered fiscal relief for the states; a negative income tax, which would reduce administrative confusion for the states and limit bureaucratic intrusiveness for the poor; and standardized benefit levels, for which a general equity argument could be made. But, perhaps most important, FAP offered the federal government greater control over welfare costs. It is significant that the reform package was developed to fit the Nixon Administration's "bottom line"—a $2 billion ceiling on welfare costs.[7]

Although crises supposedly make good politics by providing the urgency to overcome obstacles and objections, they also give issues greater visibility and political importance. For this and other reasons fully elaborated elsewhere,[8] the Administration was unable to fashion a stable legislative majority around FAP. This failure was indicative not only of FAP's particular flaws but also of the more general difficulties inherent in the legislative route to welfare reform. These included fundamental disagreements over the direction reform should take as well as the weakness of Congress as an institution for resolving these disagreements. Similar difficulties helped to wreck the Carter Administration's welfare reform efforts years later. If even the specter of a welfare crisis were insufficient to overcome obstacles to legislative policymaking, perhaps they could be overcome through alternative means.

## Changing the Arena of Conflict

Frustrated by Congress, the Nixon Administration in its second term shifted from a legislative to a managerial strategy to assert its interests in welfare and other areas.[9] From a tactical standpoint, this strategy made effective use of existing executive authority, reconstituting the HEW bureaucracy to bring it into closer alignment with the Administration's policy preferences. The strategy also decoupled highly politicized programmatic issues from apparently nonpolitical issues of managerial efficiency and financial accountability. Interests that mobilized around poverty issues during the legislative battle over welfare reform were not as engaged by "administrative politics," reducing the Administration's need to make tradeoffs and avoiding the obstacles that produced legislative stalemate.

### Reorganizing HEW

The managerial strategy and its intent have been carefully detailed by Ronald Randall. He states that President Nixon:

faced with few legislative achievements, and concluding that "operations is policy," . . . switched to a managerial strategy to change policy.

... A new set of management-oriented leaders replaced another set which had been implementing a traditional federal welfare policy distasteful to the administration. These new leaders wasted little time in employing management techniques to turn welfare policy in a restrictive, sometimes punitive, direction. (Randall, 1979, p. 808)

The first step in implementing this strategy was to replace HEW Secretary Robert Finch and his "liberal" subordinates with Caspar W. Weinberger and other noted "hardliners." Weinberger earned his reputation as "Cap the Knife" in opposing spending for social programs as head of the Office of Management and Budget (OMB) and, before that, as a participant in then-Governor Ronald Reagan's attack on welfare in California. His protégé James S. Dwight was installed as head of the Social and Rehabilitation Service (SRS), which administered welfare programs. There he quickly became known as "Attila the Hun" (Randall, 1979, pp. 797–798).

In addition to changes at the top of the agency, other less visible changes permeated the bureaucracy and altered the balance of influences. First, management staff supplanted social welfare professionals, in both number and influence. Second, bureaucratic enclaves associated with traditional agency constituencies (such as social workers and state welfare managers) were downgraded, dismantled, or bypassed in routing decisionmaking. Third, decentralization of administrative functions to regional offices reinforced growing tendencies among bureaucrats responsible for policymaking and oversight to make "end runs" around programmatic units staffed primarily by careerists with traditional biases toward welfare programs (Randall, 1979, pp. 802–804). Fourth, quality control began to take shape as an instrument for indirectly influencing welfare policy.[10]

### The Transformation of Quality Control

Although quality control had been used in social welfare administration since 1963, its impact was relatively insignificant. Until 1970, quality control was the name given to an annual case action survey, which states were to make to determine positive and negative case errors.[11] (Positive case errors included overpayments and payments to ineligibles. Negative case errors included incorrectly denied or terminated benefits.) Throughout the sixties, those surveys indicated excess payments in only 1 to 2 percent of cases sampled.

Skeptical of those findings as welfare rolls soared in the latter part of the decade, House Ways and Means Committee Chairman Wilbur Mills requested a review of New York City's welfare caseload. HEW's review of the active caseload, in contrast to its review of only those cases in which action had been taken, uncovered a case ineligibility rate of 10.7 percent (Mills, 1981, p. 79). These findings and mounting concern over growing welfare rolls prompted HEW to issue new quality control regulations in

October 1970. These regulations required states to review semi-annually a representative sample of their active cases and, for the first time, established "tolerance levels" for the proportion of cases found to contain errors. Tolerance levels were set at 3 percent for ineligible cases, 5 percent for overpaid cases, and 5 percent for underpaid cases. (A negative case action review of the accuracy of decisions to discontinue assistance also was mandated and a 3 percent error guideline established.) In addition, HEW hired Westat Research, Inc., to evaluate these "rule of thumb" guidelines and establish a basis for national error standards.

The new regulations notwithstanding, little had occurred to demonstrate serious interest in quality control as a management tool. States were erratic in meeting the requirements of semi-annual caseload reviews, and HEW efforts to obtain compliance were limited. However, at OMB, officials were scrutinizing the HEW budget, searching for ways to get control over "uncontrollable" entitlements in lieu of legislative reform. Error rates presented an obvious target. From the budget analyst's viewpoint, caseload error rates represented more than an indicator of inadequate state management practices. They signaled an unnecessary outflow of federal dollars, attributable to insufficient state interest in tightening welfare administration.

According to Randall, OMB's associate director for human resources, Paul O'Neill, met to discuss the budget for fiscal year 1973 with Frank DeGeorge, newly appointed by President Nixon to bring tighter financial management to SRS. They agreed that it was time to "do something" about quality control error rates and to pressure the states into taking action to reduce errors. Although states arguably had their own incentives to contain welfare's growth, DeGeorge and others suspected that some errors were tacitly encouraged because they shifted the poor from state-funded general assistance programs to the federally subsidized AFDC program.[12] DeGeorge is quoted in another account as asserting that states were disinterested in quality control because "the more people they had on public assistance, the less people they had on general assistance. In getting someone on public assistance, at least half of the cost would be picked up which was obviously one of those things that motivated the growth in the caseload" (Jernigan, 1980, p. 3).

## The Emergence of Quality Control as a Strategic Weapon

The Nixon appointees at OMB and HEW quickly recognized quality control's potential as an instrument for bringing states into line with the Administration's objective of containing social spending. DeGeorge proposed using quality control as a weapon against recalcitrant states by assessing fiscal penalties on the basis of state error rates. He reasoned that by holding states fiscally accountable for errors above tolerance limits, quality control would force states to curtail excessive leniency in distributing welfare benefits (Jernigan, 1980, pp. 3–4).[13] HEW General Counsel Wilmot Hastings pushed the sanctions issue even farther on legal grounds. He advised that sanctions be applied against any errors, on the basis of a zero error rate, because the agency's tolerance levels were legally indefensible.

Not surprisingly, when proposed regulations for AFDC and Medicaid were published, the zero error-based sanctions provisions drew an outraged reaction from the states. In response, HEW Secretary Elliot Richardson agreed to replace the zero error provisions with penalties based on the old tolerance levels of 3 percent for ineligible cases and 5 percent for overpaid cases.

The sanctions regulations approved by Richardson were promulgated in the first months of the Weinberger administration at HEW. As its originators anticipated, these April 1973 regulations drew the attention of HEW administrators and staff, governors, and state welfare directors to quality control error rates. However, efforts to overturn or at least ameliorate the agency's sanctions policy, rather than to comply with or enforce it, absorbed much of their energy.

## Internal and External Negotiations

Within HEW there was disagreement over how tough the agency should be on the states. Traditionally, HEW bureaucrats tended to view state welfare agencies as their constituents. In those departments that worked closely with state bureaucrats, there was a strong orientation toward preserving a cooperative relationship. These interests were expressed in minor technical adjustments that softened the blow of the sanctions regulations. For example, the regulations were modified to permit sanctions to be calculated at the lower boundary of the state error estimate and granted an "administrative lag period," during which changes in client circumstances that produced payment errors would be disregarded (Mills, 1981, p. 56). But, despite these minor concessions, HEW remained committed to a tough sanctions policy.

The states, in a weak bargaining position at HEW, moved to counteract the sanctions threat by transferring the conflict to the courts. A private study commissioned by HEW and published just before the sanctions regulations provided ammunition to the states in attacking the tolerance levels that Hastings had warned were legally indefensible. According to the study by Westat Inc., these error limits could not rationally be justified. Westat suggested that HEW establish a 9 percent tolerance level for overpaid cases, while moving gradually toward a standard based on payment rather than case errors. The study recommended that states work toward achieving a combined payment error rate of 5 percent (combining overpayments and payments to ineligibles).

Immediately after the April 1973 regulations based on 3 and 5 percent tolerance levels were issued, Ohio and Georgia filed suit against HEW in U.S. District Court in Washington, challenging the agency's authority to impose fiscal sanctions and questioning the basis on which it threatened to disallow state expenditures. In January 1975, this suit was incorporated into *Maryland v. Mathews* and joined by 13 other states and Los Angeles County. HEW General Counsel John Rhinelander advised Weinberger to postpone sanctions due in June 1975 on the grounds that the error rates on which they were based were statistically unsound and would not hold up in court. His advice proved correct. Although no sanctions had been imposed, the court in 1976 overturned the regulations on the grounds that the tolerance levels had been set "in an arbitrary and capricious manner" and constituted an "abuse of agency discretion."

### Re-opening Talks with the States

The states' victory in court was only one element in a new climate affecting the sanctions conflict in the mid-seventies. The Nixon Administration's managerial strategy was aborted as the Watergate proceedings diverted Executive attention and, ultimately, led to the President's resignation. The concerted assault on welfare ceased with the change in administrations, and interest in quality control sanctions temporarily diminished. However, the issue of controlling welfare costs remained high on the political agenda.

Although HEW Secretary F. David Mathews adopted a more conciliatory posture toward the states than his predecessors, his policy options were constrained by continuing congressional pressure on HEW to tighten state welfare administration and reduce costs. Mathews instructed SRS to prepare to implement disallowances pending a review of all penalties available to the agency. He also directed William Morrill, assistant secretary for planning and evaluation, to open negotiations with the states on quality control policy.[14]

In order to conduct formal negotiations, HEW needed to identify a single body with which it could bargain. Informal talks between the agency and states led to the creation of the New Coalition, an umbrella group for organizations that had a stake in the quality control regulations. With the National Governors' Conference assuming the lead role, other members of the coalition included the National Association of Counties, National Conference of State Legislatures, the National League of Cities, U.S. Conference of Mayors, and the American Public Welfare Association.

Notably absent from the negotiating coalition were members of organizations representing recipients of public welfare. They were non-participants, despite the often-stated argument by opponents of sanctions that sanctions would most hurt the poor. States contended that they would be forced to reduce welfare benefits and limit eligibility in order to recoup the financial loss inflicted by sanctions.

Although some acknowledged recipients to be the chief victims of this HEW policy, several factors were working against their inclusion in the sanctions negotiations. First, the issue had high visibility and immediacy for state welfare managers, whereas it seemed relatively remote as a focus for recipient activism. Second, welfare rights organizations that had thrived earlier had weakened and did not press for inclusion. Other advocacy groups, such as the Center for Social Welfare Policy and Law, recognized many of quality control's implications for their clients but had higher priorities and limited resources.[15] Legal advocates and the National Welfare Rights Organization did join forces contesting one aspect of the quality control issue. They filed suit in 1975 to force HEW to resume its review of negative case actions. These are actions taken to deny or terminate benefits. In June 1976, HEW agreed to conduct the negative case action reviews, which it had discontinued in 1973.[16]

However, the states were directly affected by sanctions and, because of the potential fiscal impact, gave the issue high priority. The states' representatives in the New Coalition formally declared sanctions non-negotiable. They argued that sanctions interfered with the state-federal partnership, would push states to reduce welfare benefits, and would unfairly penalize states for administrative problems created by complex and continually changing federal laws.

### A Short-Lived Compromise

Despite this official stance, by the end of the Ford Administration, the talks between HEW and the New Coalition had produced compromise regulations, which retained fiscal sanctions but liberalized the basis on which they would be imposed. The compromise regulations based sanctions on the percentage of payments (rather than cases) in error and established a tolerance level for overpayments to ineligibles equal to the 75th percentile of state performance in the prior period. In addition, HEW conceded on several technical points, agreeing to raise from five to ten dollars the threshold at which a payment error would be counted as an error and disregarding "paper" errors, such as failure to record a social security number or verify registration in the WIN (work training) program.[17] In addition, HEW promised to increase funding for technical assistance to the states.

In January 1977, just before the compromise regulations were to be published in the Federal Register, Pres. Carter took office. Newly-installed HEW Secretary Joseph Califano, as one of his first acts, withdrew the proposed rules and re-opened negotiations with the New Coalition. Although new regulations were not to be issued for more than two years, the quality control conflict intensified during this period as part of a renewed battle to define "the welfare problem" and national social policy.

## The Issues Are Joined

Califano entered office with a mandate to submit a comprehensive welfare reform proposal to the President by May. In the reform package he developed for the Carter Administration, as in FAP, management and benefits issues were packaged to forge a winning coalition in Congress. The Carter welfare reform proposal attempted to create a legislative majority around issues of state fiscal relief, an income tax credit,[18] and job creation. Unlike the Nixon proposals, the Carter Administration's Program for Better Jobs and Income (PBJI) reflected a more positive view of the federal government's social welfare role.

### The Political Climate

However, the climate for "liberal" welfare reform was worse, if anything, than it had been in the early seventies. Economic issues dominated much of the political agenda, with the message of Proposition 13 echoing loudly through Capitol Hill corridors. According to public opinion polls, welfare expenditures were the primary target of those seeking to reduce taxes.[19]

Rather than contest the popular notion that welfare programs were poorly managed, Califano sought to use that perception to promote comprehensive reform. Early in his administration, Califano was quoted as saying:

> I'd like to demonstrate to the American people that HEW can be managed. . . . The importance of that is to show that we can make investments in social services and social programs for the most vulnerable in society in an efficient way, as well as a compassionate way, that it is worthwhile, that government can indeed do a lot of these things and that government should indeed do a lot of these things. (Califano, quoted in *National Journal,* June 24, 1977)

As in previous reform attempts, the legislative conflict over welfare's "proper" role mobilized opposing and seemingly irreconcilable interests. Whitman's analysis of the Carter reform attempt is hauntingly similar to Marmor and Rein's conclusions regarding FAP's defeat nearly a decade earlier. On the Carter effort, Whitman comments that:

> critics of the system were united in their distaste for the "mess," but they were by no means united in their views of "reform," which in fact meant very different things to different people. The political spectrum of welfare reform included powerful congressional conservatives, welfare rights organizations, labor unions, academicians, administrators of welfare programs, and financially hard-pressed state and local governments. (Whitman, 1979, p. A-3)

While Califano sought to make comprehensive welfare reform the battleground for conflict over welfare, related disputes were occurring simultaneously on two other fronts. On one front, HEW was still occupied in continuing negotiations with the states over the quality control system and federal fiscal sanctions. On another, HEW's congressional opponents were pushing for a tougher sanctions policy and threatening to cut the HEW budget. Each of these battles became linked as interests jockeyed to improve their bargaining positions through 1978 and 1979.

### Califano's Strategy

In pursuing welfare reform. Califano attempted to juggle the interests of purported enemies of welfare fraud and waste, poor people's advocates, and beleaguered state welfare managers. Participants in the decade-long quality control conflict were divided on the merits of his strategy. "There is no question that he was an advocate of the recipients," said a former top HEW official (interview, 1982). According to this view, Califano reasoned that social programs were in jeopardy because management was too lax. Therefore, the solution was to demonstrate a tough approach to state welfare management.[20] However, the official added that Califano, in displaying his concern over poor management, "conveyed an exaggerated notion of how much fraud, waste and abuse there was in the program."

Another former official and close associate of Califano contends that the secretary "got caught in a trap" (interview, 1982). He focused on fraud and mismanagement in an effort to demonstrate that HEW was responding to congressional concerns. He believed that Congress would be more sympathetic to social spending if it perceived that HEW was moving to clean up its programs. Higher error rates, this official explained, "could be used in Congress as an excuse for not doing anything more to help these programs." This strategy led Califano into a "trap"—the rhetoric of fraud, waste, and abuse was apparently a more potent weapon for cutting than reforming social programs.

### The Inspector General's Report

The potency of the "fraud, waste, and abuse" argument increased dramatically with the March 1978 report of the HEW inspector general. The report alleged that the agency lost $6 billion to $7 billion annually as a result of mismanagement and cheating. The fact that only $600 million of the total loss was in AFDC and the bulk was in student loans and health provider fraud was overlooked in the furor that followed the report's publication.

The conservative Senate Finance Committee moved to force HEW into action and circulated its own quality control proposal. The prospect that tough sanctions would be legislatively, rather than administratively, mandated worried the counsel to the New Coalition, who cautioned his clients against provoking legislative sanctions. He contended that it would be easier to alter administrative regulations or, if necessary, to contest them in court.

Thus, the states acquired an interest in helping Califano try to divert growing congressional demands for budget cuts and stiff sanctions. He proposed new quality control regulations and announced a "crackdown" on welfare mismanagement.[21] The proposed regulations, published in July 1978, reinstated sanctions for the first time since the 1976 *Maryland v. Mathews* decision. After two years of negotiations within the agency and with the New Coalition, the regulations

- established an annual national error rate standard for AFDC and Medicaid;
- provided that the standard would be equal to the proportion of excess dollars spent nation-wide in the previous year; and
- imposed sanctions on erroneous payments in excess of the standard unless a state had reduced its payment errors at a prescribed rate, which was based on the national rate of improvement since 1975, or was unable to meet the standard because of circumstances beyond management's control.[22]

Califano's highly publicized crackdown on state welfare management was accompanied by a Six State Strategy, which provided additional technical assistance to those states accounting for the largest share of erroneously spent dollars.

### Michel and the Budget Weapon

HEW's most powerful opponent, Congressman Robert Michel (R-Ill.) was not to be diverted. Michel expressed shock at the inspector general's findings and, moreover, was unimpressed by the agency's efforts to improve program management. Despite Califano's public gestures, Michel did not believe that HEW was about to get tough with the states. As one Michel aide described the Congressman's views: "HEW let the state welfare people lead them around by the nose. . . . We were going through a runaround with them. . . . When you see error rates in the double digit range and they tell you it's hundreds of millions going down the drain, it's time to do something" (interview, 1982).

As ranking minority member of the HEW-Labor Appropriations Subcommittee, Michel amended HEW's budget for fiscal year 1979 cutting $1 billion from the total. The cuts were to be realized through management "savings" in areas cited by the inspector general and reported to Congress. Michel's across-the-board cut in the agency's budget extended the scope of conflict beyond the Administration's reform legislation or quality control sanctions.

The secretary responded that $1 billion in management savings were already incorporated in the agency's budget request and, therefore, the cuts were redundant. When Michel insisted on evidence of fresh savings, Califano asserted that if he were forced to cut $1 billion, HEW would be unable to reimburse states for AFDC and Medicaid expenditures in the final quarter of fiscal year 1979. As the argument continued into the fall of 1978 and spring of 1979, each side sought independent support for its position. While awaiting opinions from the General Accounting Office (sought by Michel) and the Justice Department (sought by HEW), Califano submitted a new welfare reform package, which was received with little enthusiasm or interest in Congress (Whitman, 1979, pp. S-22–23).

In May 1979 the comptroller general directed HEW to implement the budget cuts, followed in June by a Justice Department opinion that the cuts could be averted by borrowing against the agency's appropriation for fiscal year 1980. Nevertheless, in a carefully orchestrated strategy, Califano notified states that AFDC and Medicaid reimbursements would not be forthcoming unless the Senate expressly approved the borrowing scheme. State officials descended on congressional offices, winning support for an amendment to HEW's supplemental appropriation that granted borrowing authority.

During the House-Senate conference on the supplemental appropriation, the comptroller general issued a second opinion concurring with the Justice Department that HEW could borrow from its appropriation for fiscal year 1980 without congressional action. When Senator Warren Magnuson (D-Wash.) withdrew the Senate borrowing amendment as superfluous, Michel substituted an amendment, referred to on the Hill as "the fraud, waste, and abuse amendment." It directed HEW to use quality control sanctions to attain the management savings specified in the budget.

***The Michel "Amendment."*** The Michel "Amendment" directed HEW to issue regulations requiring states to achieve a maximum payment error rate of 4 percent in AFDC and Medicaid by fiscal year 1982.[23] In the interim, states were to improve their error rates by one-third each year in order to avoid sanctions. The secretary was directed to publish final regulations implementing these provisions no later than November 30, 1979.

The conference report reflected the opposing congressional interests at issue in the budget and sanctions debate. It stated:

> The Conferees wish to make it clear to both the HEW and the states, that under no circumstances are any payments to legitimate recipients to be curtailed or even delayed. The entitlements due eligible recipients under any programs cited by the Inspector General have never been at issue. It is the fraud, abuse and waste in those programs that must be reduced to an absolute minimum. That effort demands the attention of Federal and State agencies, and the conferees will insist it be given a higher priority by those officials than their actions to date would indicate. (Congressional Record, H 5778, July 11, 1979)

While the conference specified quality control as the mechanism for monitoring and penalizing wasteful state spending, no such provisions existed to implement the committee's concern that eligible recipients receive their entitlements fully and without delay.

*The Legislative Background.* Michel's already considerable strength and influence with regard to this issue derived from a number of factors, not the least of which was his seniority in the House and on the HEW-Labor Appropriations Subcommittee. Furthermore, Michel's intense interest was effectively converted into legislative action through the committee process, in which a single individual's influence may easily outweigh that individual's voting strength, and through his choice of fraud, waste, and abuse as the ground on which to attack the HEW budget. Staff aides to other congressmen, who later tried unsuccessfully to eliminate the Michel provisions, explained his success in the following terms: "It's so easy to demagogue this issue" or "To be against the Michel Amendment was to be against reducing fraud and abuse." Furthermore, as one staff member to the House Ways and Means Committee explained: "The Michel thing kind of came out of the blue. . . . We were looking for any way you could to save money. Once it was proposed to cut $1 billion from the HEW budget, the conference 'compromise' on sanctions seemed reasonable" (interviews, 1982).

Nevertheless, congressional counterstrategies were attempted, including an effort to replace the Michel provisions with more lenient sanctions provisions. The alternative sanctions legislation was attached in the House as an amendment to Carter's second welfare reform bill. However, the legislation, promoted by Democratic and Republican legislators from the major urban, high error states, was derailed along with welfare reform.

# A Legacy of "Fraud, Waste, and Abuse"

Califano resigned as HEW secretary in July 1979 and was replaced by Patricia Harris. Along with the position, she inherited what one close associate called the "Califano legacy of fraud, waste, and abuse." Before Harris could direct attention to her own policy agenda, she would have to diffuse the congressional attack on agency program management. The first test of the agency's commitment to dealing toughly with mismanagement occurred in September. Eleven states failed to meet their AFDC error rate targets, and 18 states failed to meet their Medicaid targets.

Harris and her top advisors viewed the prospect of widespread sanctions with distress. On the one hand, they feared that states would respond to fiscal penalties by reducing welfare benefit levels. On the other hand, they feared that other HEW social programs would be jeopardized if the agency failed to demonstrate a strong response to high error rates. Furthermore, the prospects for finding a way out of this dilemma appeared to be worsening for several reasons.

First, issues of the agency's performance in reducing error rates and funding for other social programs were becoming closely linked in the appropriation process. In the fall, Michel had successfully amended the HEW appropriations bill for the 1980 fiscal year to require $500 million in savings through management improvements and implementation of a sanctions policy based on a 4 percent error rate standard.

Second, because of the Michel Amendment, HEW would have to adopt tough new quality control regulations. Under these regulations, more states would be squeezed by fiscal sanctions, and the size of the federal penalty would also increase. In January 1980, HEW issued its new rules, which

- required states to reduce their quality control error rates (for overpayments and payments to ineligibles) to 4 percent by fiscal year 1982;
- set interim targets requiring states to progress one-third of the way to the 4 percent standard each fiscal year beginning in fiscal year 1980; and
- permitted the secretary to waive sanctions if a state had made a "good faith effort" but fell short of achieving its error target.

Third, the sanctions dilemma was complicated by the fact that the states had not shown much progress in reducing their error rates in the absence of a sanctions threat.[24] Unless states moved rapidly and effectively to reduce error, the secretary's options for responding to congressional pressure would shrink. Clearly the long-term resolution of this dilemma lay in reducing state error rates, which would relieve congressional pressure and limit the negative effects of fiscal penalties. In the short term, the sanctions threat could be useful in spurring state action, although the imposition of fiscal penalties was regarded by many in the agency as undesirable.

The conditions that existed at the start of Harris's tenure as HEW secretary produced an ironic result. Not since Caspar Weinberger's assault on welfare had there been such intense interest in pressuring states to reduce their error rates. Weinberger's administration had developed the quality control system as an instrument for getting the states to be more restrictive in distributing federal welfare dollars. But it was not until seven years later that a liberal, Democratic administration actively sought to use quality control to force states to reduce errors. Paradoxically, the rationale of the Harris administration in using this instrument was to avoid reductions in state welfare benefits and congressional funding of social programs. This irony did not entirely escape some of Harris's top staff members, one of whom later acknowledged that in helping to create a quality control system and endow it with legitimacy, "we created a monster" (interview, 1982).[25]

As the system regularly produced indicators of wasteful "errors" in welfare delivery, the error rate became a valuable weapon in the arsenal of those in Congress who sought to restrict the provision of welfare. The congressional attack on social spending was experienced by HEW in part as an "error rate crisis," and this crisis was transmitted to the states through quality control and the threat of fiscal sanctions.[26]

# 4

# Evaluating "Quality" in Welfare Delivery

As a management tool, quality control had the manifest purpose of enabling HEW to hold states accountable for administrative practices, which federal authorities could not directly control. The issue of fiscal sanctions was widely discussed among state and federal officials, consultants, and, on occasion, social welfare advocates. At times, technical design questions were also raised. However, the political values implicit in quality control measurement generally received little explicit attention. Nevertheless, quality control, like other program measures, reflected a particular weighting of political values.

As one prominent methodologist has observed: "The more any quantitative social indicator is used for social decision-making, the more subject it will be to corruption pressures and the more apt it will be to distort and corrupt the social processes it is intended to monitor" (Campbell, 1975, p. 35). In the case of quality control, the error rate indirectly influenced welfare policy-as-delivered by specifying the attributes of performance for which states would be held accountable. It is an elementary proposition of organizational behavior that organizations will maximize production of measured attributes of performance, other things being equal.[1] Given this tendency, the content and validity of a performance measure has more than academic interest. Political biases or technical deficiencies in the measure may affect agency behavior with undesirable consequences for the production of public policy. An intermediate step in understanding quality control's indirect influence on welfare policy-as-delivered involves an assessment of the measurement system itself in both its political and technical dimensions. A brief description of this system and how it operated at the time of this study sets the background for this assessment.

41

## The Quality Control Process

The quality control review process involves a semi-annual assessment of a sample of each state's active AFDC caseload. Approximately 45,000 cases are randomly selected for review nationwide, with the sample size varying from about 150 to 1,200 cases, depending on the size of each state's caseload. Each state welfare agency has its own quality control unit, which checks the accuracy of sampled cases by conducting a full field investigation of recipient eligibility. Based on an HEW-designed format, which is adapted to fit variations in state welfare policy, reviewers verify some 45 elements of eligibility to determine whether the payment issued in the review month was accurate; that is, it did not overpay or underpay the recipient by more than five dollars.[2] Based on these reviews, the state agency produces an estimate of its error rate—the dollars overpaid or paid to ineligible persons as a percentage of total payments—which is used as the basis for fiscal sanctions. A separate underpayment rate is also produced but is not subject to fiscal penalties.

A sub-sample of the state sample is reviewed by federal quality control staff in each of HEW's regional offices. Based on the re-review, the state's estimate of excess payments is adjusted according to the federal estimate of erroneous state quality control decisions. The rate at which the state reviewers undercounted excess payments is extrapolated to the entire state caseload by a formula that determines the final, adjusted error rate. This formula, intended to correct state underestimates, has the effect of multiplying each new error that is discovered in the federal review by several times (with the precise amount dependent on the sample size). For example, in Massachusetts, a $300 per month overpayment that is discovered in the federal re-review translates into $600,000 in potential fiscal sanctions when extrapolated to the state's error rate for the six-month review period.

## Political Values and Design Issues

Assuming that it is desirable to pay benefits only to those eligible for assistance and to make payments in accordance with statutory and regulatory provisions, what are the attributes of payment "accuracy" that might be measured to assess state administrative performance? The Urban Institute prepared a comprehensive report to HEW in 1978 on this and other related questions. It recommended that, in addition to overpayments and payments to ineligibles, quality control incorporate underpayments into the error rate for which states were held accountable. Moreover, it advised HEW to incorporate a measure of erroneous nonpayments and impediments to access by potential recipients. The report suggested a preliminary design for such a measure, which it called an "index of accessibility." The index comprised measures of processing delays, procedural deterrents to applicants (such as long waiting lines), the rate of non-participation by potential recipients, appeals to administrative fair hearings, and the rate at which benefits were denied or terminated for procedural noncompliance (Bendick et al., 1978, pp. 160–161).

The authors of the report stressed their concern that "in the search for error reduction" HEW might "unduly sacrifice" the objective of making welfare accessible to families entitled to assistance. They reminded HEW that "after all, the AFDC program exists for the purpose of providing income assistance to over 11 million low-income persons unable to support themselves, and this purpose should not be forgotten in a comprehensive program of quality control" (Bendick et al., 1978, p. 36). Their recommendations for a "countervailing force" to balance "inordinate sacrifice of client accessibility" were distinctive in the level of technical supporting detail supplied. However, they shared the fate of other similar proposals and generated no apparent interest at HEW.

### Measuring Nonpayment Errors

In contrast, the National Welfare Rights Organization got HEW's attention and a concrete response, with a court suit to force HEW to resume so-called negative case action (NCA) reviews that had been discontinued in 1973. HEW agreed in 1977 to require states to conduct NCA reviews, although the requirement was not vigorously enforced. But, for several reasons, the NCA reviews did not effectively provide the "countervailing force" envisioned by their advocates.

Three methodological distinctions between the regular quality control review and the NCA review undermined the latter's value as a measure of erroneous nonpayment. First, in the regular quality control review, checks for accuracy involved a de novo field investigation, including interviews with recipients and independent verification of information (for example, through public school and municipal records, banks, and even neighbors and work associates). In contrast, the NCA review involved only an in-house appraisal of case records to determine whether information in the case file supported the reason given for the agency's decision to terminate or deny benefits. This type of review is, of course, faster and cheaper than a full-scale quality control review. But it could not determine whether the agency's decision was correct with respect to the "facts," which Mashaw had assumed to be an essential condition of "accuracy."

Second, the NCA review produced an estimate of the cases improperly denied as a percentage of all denials, but it did not estimate the dollar "savings" accrued to the state by nonpayment. Thus, the NCA error rate could not be compared with the payment error rate.

Third, the NCA review did not indicate whether administrative procedures discouraged potential recipients from seeking assistance or completing applications for welfare. Mendeloff (1977) has referred to nonpayments that occur for these reasons as "preventive errors," because potential quality control errors are avoided by preventing potential claimants from gaining access to the system.

Measurement of NCAs and underpayments notwithstanding, HEW's failure to hold states accountable for underpayments and nonpayments had prima facie political significance. When pressed, HEW officials have defended the quality control system's design on the grounds that the agency lacked administrative authority to hold states fiscally accountable for failing to pay benefits to which families were entitled. They have argued that this design was, in part, dictated by the tools at their disposal, namely, the agency's authority to withhold reimbursements for erroneous state expenditures.[3] Regardless of one's judgment of this argument, the quality control system as implemented by HEW has been "clearly more concerned with saving the government money than providing welfare to people who qualify," as one expert witness told a congressional committee back in 1973 (Lurie, 1973, p. 100).

### The Practical Significance of Quality Control's Design

In contrast to other evaluation mechanisms used by HEW, such as annual field reviews of state welfare administration, quality control's practical significance derives from the following distinctive features. First, it focuses strictly on the accuracy of welfare payments—particularly overpayments and payments to ineligibles—rather than on a more comprehensive set of administrative concerns.[4] Second, the payment error rate regularly produced by the quality control system can be used to specify the extent of payment errors, improvement or deterioration in state payment accuracy, and comparative performance among states. Third, when a state's error rate falls below its "tolerance" threshold, the sanctions process is automatically triggered, placing the state in a defensive posture in arguing for a waiver of fiscal penalties.

The practical significance of these features was recognized by Mendeloff, who in a 1977 study questioned whether state interest in minimizing "errors of liberality" (which were subject to fiscal sanctions) could result in the creation of "errors of stringency." Errors of liberality refer to overpayments and payments to ineligible persons and errors of stringency to underpayments and nonpayments. Mendeloff contended that HEW's singular concern with errors of liberality implied that "underpayment error can be adequately controlled by relying on welfare officials' adherence to regulations, on the self-interest of clients, and on review of the courts." Alternatively, he hypothesized that administrative reforms implemented to reduce quality control errors would create errors that would "victimize" recipients (Mendeloff, 1977, p. 358).

In the absence of data on nonpayments, Mendeloff sought to test whether administrative practices in 14 California counties had resulted in a tradeoff between the two types of measured errors (all excess payments and underpayments). His findings suggested that such a tradeoff did occur and indicated that an improvement in the quality control error rate did not mean an improvement in administrative performance generally. To the extent that other evidence exists on the question of an error tradeoff, it generally supports Mendeloff's hypothesis. For example, Piliavin et al. (1979) examined worker and organizational characteristics associated with quality control errors. Almost incidentally, they found that workers who tended to make more of one type of error made fewer of the other type of error.

Mills's study of the error rate problem was unusual in assuming that a tradeoff between types of error was an intrinsic feature of welfare administration. He hypothesized that because of the marginal cost of reducing either errors of liberality or errors of stringency, efforts made to reduce one type of error—without any increase in "productive input"—would increase errors of the other type (Mills, 1981, pp. 113–114). Based on an analysis of quality control data from all states and the District of Columbia for review periods between July 1975 and December 1977, he found that in the aggregate overpayments and underpayments were negatively correlated. However, Mills did not attempt to determine the full extent to which errors of stringency, including nonpayments, occurred. This question is likely to remain unanswered in the absence of usable quality control data on erroneous nonpayments.

In sum, the definition of administrative accuracy embodied in the quality control error rate involved an unacknowledged tradeoff between objectives of cost containment and the provision of benefits to those entitled to assistance. In this sense, quality control was not a neutral management tool but arguably an instrument for achieving particular political objectives. Moreover, it had the potential for influencing state agencies, indirectly, to trade errors of liberality for errors of stringency in reforming their administrative procedures to maximize quality control performance.

## Problems in Measurement Validity

The preceding discussion examines the terms on which quality control defined payment accuracy and the political meaning of those terms. However, the validity of the error rate as a measure of state administrative performance can also be questioned on its own terms—as an indicator of excess payments. Recent studies by the General Accounting Office (GAO) (1980) and Mills (1981) suggest at least two areas in which the conditions necessary to validity appear to be unsatisfied.[5]

According to Campbell, "of the threats to external validity, the one most relevant to social experimentation is irrelevant responsiveness of measures" (Campbell, 1973, p. 200). A single measure is apt to capture effects caused by factors other than the presumed independent variable (in this case administrative improvements), making variation in the measure difficult to interpret.[6] One solution is to consider other factors that may cause variation in the measure. Available evidence, summarized as follows, suggests that the error rate responds to a variety of influences that have little or no bearing on administrative accuracy.

### Irrelevant Responsiveness

First, the error rate is a function of differences in the quality control review process. Differences include the extent to which reviewers probe into elements of eligibility, the evidence they accept as verification, and the scope of their investigations (for example, whether they interview a recipient's neighbors or employer). The GAO studied the review process in five states and five HHS regional offices and concluded that it differed "from state to state and federal region to region" (U.S. Congress, General Accounting Office, 1980, p. ii). Moreover, federal officials did not apply consistent standards in evaluating state review processes. The GAO said that it was unable to determine the extent to which these differences affected error rates but advised against using these rates for cross-state comparison.

Mills measured the effect of one difference in the quality control review process, which he labeled "intensity." He hypothesized that the smaller a reviewer's caseload, the more "intense" would be the review, increasing the probability of finding errors. Measuring intensity as the number of cases per reviewer, he examined its relationship with state error rates between the second halves of 1975 and 1977. According to his analysis, one-half of the decline in the error rate during that period could be attributed to the increased workload of federal quality control reviewers (Mills, 1981, p. 167).

Second, the error rate is a function of state welfare policy, particularly its benefits structure. States determine their benefits structure within the broad confines of federal welfare policy. They may choose to pay any portion or all of the state-established standard of need. States that pay less than the standard of need have a greater margin for error because of the way quality control measures accuracy.

The GAO offers two examples (U.S. Congress, General Accounting Office, 1980, pp. 11–12). In New York, an eligible family of four received 100 percent of the standard of need, which was $476. A quality control reviewer discovered an arithmetic error and found that the family was eligible for only $461, resulting in a $15 overpayment. In Indiana, the maximum standard of need for a family of four was $327. Because of a $275 ceiling on payments, that is what the family received. A quality control review indicated that the calculation of the family's need was inaccurate, that, in fact, it was entitled to $15 less than the $327 standard of need. But this mistake did not result in a quality control error because the actual payment of $275 was still correct. According to the GAO's review of cases in Indiana for the period from April to September 1978, 42 cases, or about one-third of the state's quality control sample, contained mistakes of this type, which were not counted in calculating the quality control error rate (U.S. Congress, General Accounting Office, 1980, pp. 11–12).

The error rate is also affected by the extent to which state welfare policy standardizes benefits. For example, a state that permits every working recipient to deduct $28 for work-related expenses tends to produce fewer errors than a state in which benefits are adjusted according to a recipient's actual work expenses. The GAO compared errors in benefits calculations in Maine and New York, the former having a standard allowance for basic family needs (called a consolidated grant) and the latter determining needs according to a basic allowance plus actual costs for shelter and utilities (a partially consolidated grant). In the quality control review period from January to June 1978, only two errors related to basic needs calculations were found in Maine's 603 case sample. In New York, there were 110 errors in its 1,238 case sample (U.S. Congress, General Accounting Office, 1980, p. 11).

State adoption of consolidated grants appears to account for a substantial decline in error rates during the mid-seventies. According to an 11–state study by Touche Ross and Company (1977), eight states that adopted consolidated grants between 1972 and 1977 showed more than a 70 percent decline in errors in the calculation of basic needs. Mills's analysis of the 1975 to 1977 period indicated that consolidated grants were associated with 21.2 percent of the national error rate decline and payment ceilings with 45.9 percent (Mills, 1981, p. 162).[7]

Third, the error rate is a function of the states' caseload characteristics. Mills hypothesized that the larger the proportion of cases with working recipients, the greater the likelihood of payment errors. Earnings cases, as they commonly are called, required detailed calculations of average wages, taxes, deductions, and work expenses. A further complication derives from the fact that the earnings and job tenure of welfare recipients are highly variable. The calculations made by a worker at the time of application or redetermination may be out-of-date by the time of a quality control review, even a few months later. Mills found that more than 10 percent of the decline in error rates nationally between 1975 and 1977 was associated with a decrease in the percentage of earnings cases (Mills, 1981, pp. 167–168).

In a performance measure, irrelevant responsiveness has implications beyond confounding attempts to make inter-state comparisons or interpret error rate variation. It also has political implications if, as Campbell predicted, indicators themselves become "the goal of social action, rather than the social problems they but imperfectly indicate" (Campbell, 1973, p. 203). State policymakers, who recognize policy's effects on error rates, may at times make policy decisions on the basis of these effects rather than other social objectives.

The GAO reported discussions with Indiana and Maine officials who were concerned that error rates would rise if their state welfare policies were liberalized to include optional programs that required relatively complicated calculations or administrative determinations. Programs specified as likely to increase the error rate included those for children aged 18 to 21 who are in specified educational or training programs, families with unemployed parents, and pregnant women who have no other children (U.S. Congress, General Accounting Office, 1980, p. 13).

### Relevancy and Reliability

In the case of quality control, the distinction between relevant and irrelevant factors is not always clear-cut. Included in the definition of inaccurate payments are so-called "paper errors," which when corrected may not alter the amount or distribution of payments. These errors became the focus of controversy in 1978, when HEW decided to count in error payments made to any person whose social security number was missing from the case record or who had failed to register for the WIN program, unless exempt. With this change in error rate measurement, HEW announced its intention to hold states accountable for implementing the 1976 Talmadge Amendment to the Social Security Act, which imposed these requirements as conditions of eligibility for AFDC. The ostensible purpose of these provisions, as mentioned earlier, was to screen from the welfare rolls "employables" and individuals with unreported earnings that made them ineligible. (Using social security numbers, welfare departments could run computer matches with banks, tax departments, and unemployment agencies.)

States argued that paper errors did not necessarily indicate payment errors, because when corrected, payments were unaffected. Nevertheless, HEW made such errors liable for fiscal sanctions on the grounds that a recipient was technically ineligible for AFDC unless these requirements were fulfilled. Ironically, the inclusion of paper errors created a short-term problem but a longer-term advantage for those states that had large numbers of paper errors. Because such errors were relatively easy to correct, states with many of them could dramatically improve their error rate scores. It was as though states had heeded Campbell's advice to "trapped administrators whose political predicament requires a favorable outcome whether valid or not." If they could pick as a base for comparison "the very worst year and the very worst social unit . . . there is nowhere to go but up" (Campbell, 1973, p. 197).

In addition to clear and unclear "irrelevancies," the validity of an indicator may also be jeopardized by changes that occur in the measurement instrument or unreliable measurement procedures. The inclusion of paper errors was one major change, but there have been others that are more difficult to adjust for when comparing error rates over time. Touche Ross and Company (1977, p. 10) estimated that 17 percent of the national error rate reduction that occurred between 1973 and 1975 was associated with changes in the federal definition of error involving administrative "lag" periods. In effect, HEW used this device to give state agencies some time (currently one month) to adjust their payments to account for changes in client eligibility. Errors that occur within the "lag" period are not counted in the error rate.

Measurement reliability was a particular target of GAO criticism in 1980. As previously noted, the GAO found substantial discrepancies in quality control review methods, concluding that "the proportion of a state's error rate that is due to administrative problems and the portion due to quality control review differences cannot be determined" (U.S. Congress, General Accounting Office, 1980, p. 13). There is also an intrinsic degree of variation among states, because payment accuracy is evaluated according to each state's welfare policies. Overall, the GAO found the error rate too unreliable and too crude an indicator to be used as a basis for fiscal sanctions.

## The "Invisible" Problem: Reviewer Discretion

Although the GAO and Mills make important contributions in identifying overt differences in state and federal quality control review processes, the more subtle effects of reviewer discretion on this process are virtually unknown. Yet, reviewer discretion poses fundamental threats to the validity and reliability of quality control measurement and has implications that are both technical and political.

In quality control reviews, as in welfare determinations, eligibility issues are frequently unclear. Because policies may be confusing or contradictory and the family circumstances to which they are applied are often complex and idiosyncratic, discretion is inherent in welfare administration. Given these intrinsic ambiguities, the attributes of an "accurate" benefits decision cannot be fully specified. Furthermore, specification involves a tradeoff between overspecification, which may lead reviewers to categorize individual cases incorrectly as accurate or erroneous, and underspecification, which may decrease the consistency and reliability of reviewers' decisions (Lax, 1978).

Essentially, reviewer discretion in performance measurement confounds efforts to ensure validity and reliability, much as bureaucratic discretion creates uncertainty and variation in policy implementation. Moreover, as bureaucratic discretion is known to shape policy-as-delivered (Lipsky, 1978), one might look for reviewer discretion to shape the "error-rate-as-applied." This analogy suggests that insights into the quality control process and the meaning of the error rate "as applied" can be gained by examining the exercise of reviewer discretion and environmental factors that shape reviewer decisions. The following analysis draws on interviews with state and federal quality control officials and observation of the work of a Boston quality control unit (in May 1982). It highlights the types of problems posed by reviewer discretion in error rate measurement and structural influences on reviewer choices in the Massachusetts Department of Public Welfare (MDPW).[8]

## The MDPW Review System

The quality control process begins within the state welfare agency. The MDPW's Office of Program Assessment (OPA) is responsible for reviewing 1,200 randomly selected AFDC cases over the course of the six-month review period. OPA employs approximately 21 AFDC reviewers, who each investigate 9 to 11 cases per month. A supervisor assigned to each unit of five reviewers checks completed cases before sending them to the central office. The assistant director for AFDC quality control then examines each error finding in preparation for a weekly meeting of the agency's "error committee," which includes quality control, operations, and policy staff. They examine case errors to determine if the reviewer overlooked evidence or policy that could alter the determination; if evidence or policy could be interpreted differently to eliminate the error; or if patterns or types of errors are occurring that could be remedied by modifying state policy or practice.

Two federal reviewers from Region One of the Social Security Administrations (SSA) Office of Assessment re-review one-seventh of the state sample (or about 185 cases). Differences (or variances, as they are called) between state and federal findings are checked by the unit chief before being sent to the state agency. In disputed cases, federal officials may accept state arguments and change their findings, or in the case of continuing disputes, the state may carry the issue to the regional SSA director or, ultimately, to Washington.

Quality control reviewers, for the most part, conduct a de novo investigation of some 45 elements of eligibility. Verification of many of these elements, which are specified in the case review manual, may be clear-cut. However, reviewers routinely exercise discretion when evidence or policy is ambiguous. For example, it is relatively simple to verify whether a family meets the categorical eligibility requirement of WIN registration. If the case record provides acceptable documentation that the children are younger than six years old (for example, certified birth certificates), the parent is clearly WIN-exempt. If records indicate that the parent is not exempt, WIN registration may be documented by a signed and dated registration form and current registration confirmed by examining the master computer file of active WIN registrants.

In contrast, one of the most difficult elements of categorical eligibility to verify is deprivation because of the father's absence. If the mother cannot establish the father's whereabouts, reviewers must decide how far and where to probe for information that would prove absence. In addition, reviewers must evaluate the credibility of evidence, such as an affidavit from a neighbor or an anonymous tip from a social worker.[9]

The review of financial eligibility requires, among other things, verification of whether a working recipient's earnings were correctly calculated and reported and whether other income sources were correctly included or excluded. Verification of earnings is relatively straightforward when the recipient can provide wage stubs covering the appropriate periods (generally three consecutive weeks during the quality control review month). However, earnings are more difficult to verify when wage stubs are not available. And the most problematic verification occurs in response to negative assertions— for example, that the recipient is not working or that members of the household are not eligible for or receiving other benefits (such as disability insurance or veterans' benefits).

A degree of ambiguity is acknowledged in the federal quality control review manual at the conclusion of 14 pages of technical specifications. When family circumstances are "difficult to document or otherwise substantiate definitively," the manual instructs:

> The full field investigation extend[s] to the point that is considered by the reviewer to be reasonable and prudent. . . . In those case situations where it is necessary to rely on types of evidence requiring judgment and interpretation, the reviewer should consult his supervisor. These situations require sound judgment to ensure the integrity of the review process. The concurrence of the QC supervisor in the decision will generally ensure that the evidence developed is adequate to reach the necessary decisions. (U.S. Department of Health, Education and Welfare, Social Security Administration, 1978, p. 19)

### Structural Incentives

Given that discretion is an intrinsic component of the quality control review, what influences reviewer decisions? As hypothesized previously, workers can be expected to make a tradeoff between the production of different types of errors, with quality control exerting a bias toward minimizing positive errors (overpayments and payments to ineligibles), which are subject to fiscal sanctions. Evidence described as follows indicates that the behavior of quality control reviewers is consistent with this hypothesis and that they tend to focus almost exclusively on positive errors but fail to investigate negative errors (especially the failure to pay benefits).

In the units I observed, reviewers tended to be disinterested in negative errors, routinely ignoring evidence pointing toward such errors in the course of their investigations. As one supervisor explained, "I don't think the 'feds' worry about those errors, so we don't. They are not sanctioned, after all." Furthermore, reviewers, who were often hard-pressed to maintain production schedules, were not inclined to acknowledge or inquire into potential negative errors. During my observation of a quality control unit, one reviewer just completing a case expressed surprise when I pointed to documents in the records indicating that a baby born prior to the review date had not been added to the household budget until seven months later. In response to my question, he mentioned this point to his supervisor, who advised him to ignore it.[10]

Although one would expect the quality control system to create disincentives to finding negative errors at the state agency level, one might also expect even stronger disincentives to finding positive errors, which are subject to fiscal sanctions. However, despite the state's interest in minimizing its error rate, disincentives to finding positive errors were not merely constrained, but reversed, by the impact of the federal formula used to adjust the state error rate. Recognizing that states would have few incentives to uncover their own errors, HEW established regional quality control units to check on the accuracy of the state's findings. The federal re-review of one-seventh of the state's sample produces an estimate of the extent to which payment errors are understated. This estimate is used to adjust the error rate produced by the state's quality control review.

As noted earlier, the adjustment formula's effect of multiplying by seven times any "errors of omission"—that is, the failure to designate errors—means that a simple omission has serious fiscal consequences. Adjustments are also made for state "errors of commission"—that is, cases deemed erroneous that federal reviewers regard as accurate. However, these errors are not subject to the multiplier but are corrected on a dollar-for-dollar basis.

The federal check on the state also assumes that reviewers may drop some of the most complicated cases, which "coincidentally" may be those most likely to contain errors.[11] Therefore, federal reviewers attempt to complete cases that have been dropped by state quality control as "unable to determine." Errors subsequently discovered by federal reviewers are adjusted on a dollar-for-dollar basis. However, the high rate of dropped cases in Massachusetts, nearly 25 percent of the sample, led federal reviewers to change tactics. In the spring of 1982, they began to return to the state for its review those cases they determined could be completed. This subjected to the multiplier dropped cases subsequently found to contain errors. These strategic maneuvers illustrate how the error rate can be responsive to bureaucratic gamesmanship.

## Quality Control Policy in Practice

In practice, the "accuracy" of state welfare payments is determined by reviewers, who exercise discretion within the context of structural incentives, such as those described previously. After a set of "decision rules" are inferred from these incentives, selected cases will be used to illustrate how these tacit rules influence the review process and shape the error-rate-as-applied.[12]

Assuming that discretion in the quality control review is influenced by a structural bias toward minimizing errors of omission, the following decision rules can be hypothesized. First, where evidence or policy is ambiguous, it is preferable to cite the case as erroneous or to drop it. Alternatively, errors of commission are constrained to the extent that the quality control director or "error committee" is willing to overturn reviewer error findings or risk the penalties for errors of omission. However, the state's uncertainty about the federal response could be expected to produce conservative decisions.[13] Furthermore, although it is relatively costless to drop cases, this alternative is constrained by the (increasing) likelihood that the case will be returned by federal quality control for completion if a re-review indicates that a determination can be made. In addition, the state faces both a loss of "good faith" and the prospect of a supplementary sample if too many cases are dropped.

Second, the possibility that federal quality control will contest ambiguous findings can be minimized by meticulously documenting all evidence and reasoning leading to the state determination. Federal reviewers are permitted to accept primary documentation (such as drivers' licenses, social security cards, certified birth certificates) without further inquiry into those elements of eligibility that they verify. In addition, federal reviewers, who, all things being equal, prefer to avoid a long and difficult investigation, may concur with an ambiguous state determination if the reasoning is explicit. For example, they may decide not to probe further into deprivation by parental absence if the state reviewer has clearly and plausibly documented the trail of evidence, conversations, and attempts to resolve ambiguities that occurred in the course of investigation. Third, in order to minimize the penalties associated with errors of omission, it is a relatively low-cost, high-benefit proposition for the state to contest federal error findings, particularly when the federal decision rests on ambiguous evidence or policy.

***Example One: The Martinez Case.*** For five years, Mrs. Martinez received AFDC for herself and her three children. Because her husband had left the home, the family was categorically eligible for assistance. Although Mrs. Martinez had cooperated with the Child Support Enforcement Unit (CSEU),[14] the MDPW had not located Mr. Martinez. At a redetermination five months before the quality control review date, Mrs. Martinez reported no changes to the local office worker.

The Martinez case was randomly selected for a state quality control review and assigned to a Spanish-speaking reviewer, Mr. Lopez. As part of the review process, Mr. Lopez sought to establish as conclusively as possible that Mr. Martinez was, in fact, an absent parent. When Mrs. Martinez's responses to questions concerning her husband "seemed weak," the reviewer pressed further. Subsequently, Mrs. Martinez admitted that her husband had returned home in December, but she was afraid to tell the welfare worker (whose English she had difficulty understanding), fearing she might lose her benefits. She explained that she could not afford to be cut off welfare, because shortly after returning home, her husband had been disabled on the job and then laid off.

Mr. Lopez (a former welfare worker) told Mrs. Martinez that she need not worry about losing her benefits and that, with additional information, he might be able to help her straighten out her record. If he could confirm that her husband returned home in December and was laid off in January, the family might retroactively lose benefits for the month of December but would be eligible for additional benefits beginning in January, when her husband should have been added to the grant.

In order to document Mr. Martinez's absence and return, Mr. Lopez checked with the Martinez employer. However, the employer contended that Mr. Martinez had lived at home before December, citing the family's address listed on work records as evidence. Mrs. Martinez was able to provide documents that verified both her husband's disability and subsequent layoff, but she could not provide evidence of his residence prior to December. On the other hand, Mr. Lopez could not conclusively establish that Mr. Martinez lived with his family before that date.

After several weeks, Mr. Lopez was no closer to resolving the case facts. His supervisor, pressing him to complete the review, offered two alternatives. One, he could find the case to be in error, if it appeared that the husband had been living at home before December. Two, if it appeared that the husband had returned home in December, the case should be found to contain a "PAL" error (an error occurring within one month of the review date), which is discounted for quality control purposes. In either case, the family would continue to be eligible for benefits and the husband added to the grant as of January 8, the date he was laid off from work.

The supervisor advised Mr. Lopez to call Mrs. Martinez one final time to ascertain her husband's November address. If she were to respond that she had tried but had been unable to obtain evidence of where he had been living, Mr. Lopez could accept her claim as the best available evidence. However, if she did not say that she had tried but failed to verify her claim, Mr. Lopez should accept the employer's work record as the best possible evidence. Mr. Lopez objected, arguing that the decision should not hinge on whether Mrs. Martinez "said the magic words."

Eager to conclude the discussion and the case, the supervisor offered to submit the matter to the assistant director for quality control, and Mr. Lopez agreed to abide by his decision. Within several minutes, the supervisor returned with the following decision from the central office. Neither the employer's nor Mrs. Martinez's assertions were sufficient to verify where the husband had lived in November. Therefore, the case should be dropped as "unable to determine," and the local office should be notified to terminate the Martinez family for "failure to cooperate with quality control." Presuming that Mrs. Martinez received a termination notice from the local office,[15] she had the following options: (1) take no action and accept the loss of AFDC and probably Medicaid; (2) file a fair hearing appeal, guaranteeing continued benefits until the hearing date; (3) try to obtain the information sought by the quality control reviewer in order to avoid a closing either by the worker or on appeal to a fair hearing referee[16] if she understood why her assistance was being terminated and could comply; or (4) reapply for benefits after at least 30 days. Before that period she would have to be reinstated by the worker who closed her case.

The Martinez case provides a stark example of one reviewer's response to cross-pressures generated by his personal concern for the recipient, the need to document the husband's absence in order to avoid an error of omission, and, finally, organizational productivity demands. It also illustrates how the preferred alternatives for resolving ambiguities in available evidence varied according to the position of the decisionmaker. In this case, the reviewer never reached his own decision. His supervisor's solution—in order to expedite the case—was to apply an informal convention to test the recipient's credibility, namely, whether she offered "the magic words." At the central office level, the final decision to drop the case reflected a high degree of aversion to risking an error of omission. It also reflected the least concern for the consequences to the Martinez family. Notably, the central office is farthest removed from interaction with recipients, who, in this case, would receive an unexpected notice of termination.

*Example Two: The Rogers Case.* Although state and federal reviewers may agree on case facts, they may reach different conclusions concerning the appropriate payment when policy is unclear or contradictory. Five-year-old George Rogers and his grandmother, Mrs. Jones, receive an AFDC grant for a two-person household. Although the child's mother, Mrs. Rogers, lived in the same household, she had given legal custody of George to his grandmother. Under an agreement with the state CSEU, which was formalized in a probate court decree, Mrs. Rogers paid $20 per month of her $290 gross monthly earnings from working as a maid to the CSEU for child support. (Her contribution went into a general state fund; George and Mrs. Jones received only their welfare grant.)

The case appeared to be a simple one. George and his grandmother had no resources other than welfare, and state quality control determined that the two-person grant was accurately paid. Federal quality control disagreed. The federal reviewer contended that Mrs. Rogers's full monthly earnings should have been attributed to the household as income. The case, therefore, was overpaid by $290 a month. The federal review cited MDPW regulation 204.330A, which stated:

> Natural or adoptive parents have a legal obligation to support their children. If the natural or adoptive parent of the child is in the home, his or her income or assets must be considered in determining the eligibility of the dependent child although the parent need not be included in the assistance unit.

This "error of omission," when factored into the error rate adjustment formula, amounted to some $600,000 in potential fiscal penalties. Because of its serious fiscal implications, state officials looked long and hard at the Rogers case when they received a list of federal quality control variances. In discussions within the state quality control division, officials considered a variety of aspects of the case. First, if the state documented that the probate court had ordered Mrs. Rogers to pay $20 a month to the state, how could federal quality control attribute her entire $290 monthly earnings to the household? At minimum, her available income was $270. Second, if one attributed all of Mrs. Rogers's resources as available to her child, how was she supposed to live? Certainly, her cost of living should be deducted from her income and only the net income regarded as available to her child.

As state officials continued to ponder the case, they found regulations that if applied, resulted in the conclusion that an error had indeed occurred, but an underpayment, not an overpayment. Regulation 304.300 stated in part that "the assistance unit and the household may or may not be the same group of persons." Regulation 304.320 added that:

[the] applicant or recipient must be informed of the advantages and disadvantages of the alternatives before she makes a decision. While inclusion in the assistance unit confers automatic eligibility for medical assistance, the income and assets of any individual who chooses to be included in the unit must be considered in determining the unit's eligibility and the grant amount.

Although the regulations were somewhat ambiguous, state officials interpreted them to allow the MDPW to include not only Mrs. Rogers's income but also Mrs. Rogers in the household grant. Once her earnings were subject to normal deductions for work expenses and the $30 plus one-third of earnings disregard (a work incentive provision), the benefits for a three-person grant (including Mrs. Rogers, George, and Mrs. Jones) would exceed the amount that was paid to the family as a two-person unit.

Having already made an error of omission, state quality control officials incurred no additional risks by contesting the federal finding. Given the high fiscal stakes, it was worth investing time in sorting out the policy puzzle until a "desirable" solution could be found. Although the state's solution would work to the benefit of the Rogers family, that outcome was largely an inadvertent consequence of the MDPW's desire to minimize the error rate. Thus, although the consequences of the state's decisions differed dramatically for the Rogers and Martinez households, in neither case were these effects influential in determining how ambiguities would be resolved. In fact, one can easily imagine that the state might have interpreted its own policies differently if it were balancing the costs of precedent against a single case error.

## The Error Rate Revisited

When discretion is a necessary component of organizational production, as it is in determining welfare benefits, performance measurement is highly problematic. Under such circumstances, performance measurement exacts a tradeoff between external validity (the relation of the product-as-specified to the product-as-desired) and reliability (variation in the measure). Moreover, when specification is imperfect, as in the case of quality control because evidence or policy may be ambiguous, measurement presents an even more fundamental difficulty. This is because, at times, there may be no "right answer" to what is an "accurate" payment that can be uniformly deduced from available evidence or policy. As one federal quality control official asserted, "We try to be precise, but chances are neither we nor the state is 'right.'"

If the "answers" to determining claims of entitlement are ambiguous, then the question of who decides what is "right" becomes critical. Before quality control was introduced, social workers in local welfare offices possessed substantial latitude in fitting policy to family circumstances in order to determine entitlements. However, subsequent to quality control, discretion to make these determinations shifted to state and federal quality control bureaucracies, which operated within a different structure of incentives and which brought a distinctive perspective to bear on decisionmaking.

In contrast to social workers, quality control reviewers operated within a system that provided powerful incentives to find errors, even to make errors of commission. Furthermore, their search for errors was not tempered by long-term relationships with clients, general casework responsibilities, or other cross-pressures that characterized the job of the welfare caseworker.

The most important influence on quality control decisionmaking was the design of the error rate measurement system. That design reflected a singular concern with excess state payments but ignored nonpayments and failed to attach sanctions even to underpayments. Through this mechanism, the objective of cost containment gained salience in state welfare agencies, almost regardless of the individual intentions of the bureaucrats who implemented the system, particularly those at the state level. Ironically, in Massachusetts, MDPW officials found that their interest in avoiding fiscal sanctions required that they be diligent, even excessive, in adjudging their own workers to have distributed benefits too liberally.

# 5

# Reform at the State Level

By the time of the federal "error rate crisis" in 1979, the system for delivering welfare benefits in Massachusetts was clearly in need of reform. The MDPW had earned a reputation as one of the most poorly managed departments in the nation. For the quality control review period from October 1978 to March 1979, the department's error rate reached a startling 24.8 percent, the second highest in the nation after Alaska. Under the terms of quality control regulations then in effect, HEW threatened to withhold $9.1 million in reimbursements. Less dramatic, but indicative of the depth of its problems, the MDPW's error rate had been one-quarter to one-third higher than the national average for most of the decade. (See Table 1.4.)

The state's problems had not appeared suddenly but had accumulated over years of rapid growth in the size and complexity of welfare programs unmatched by legislative support for organizational development to meet changing demands. The state's recipient population had nearly doubled over the course of the seventies with more than 119,000 families receiving AFDC in fiscal year 1979 at a cost of $447 million, about half of which was reimbursed by HEW. (See Table 5.1.) The seriousness of the state's problems was underscored by the fact that Massachusetts alone accounted for more than half of the dollars HEW threatened to withhold from states in the spring of 1979.

Thus, although administrative problems were not unique to Massachusetts, their severity and the size of the state's welfare program made them particularly acute. From almost any perspective, there were strong arguments to be made for reform. Millions of dollars were being lost or wasted. Those in need of assistance could not be assured of receiving accurate and timely benefits. Workers were demoralized by the daily pressures of coping with the administrative "mess." Furthermore, if HEW were to re-

58

**Table 5.1**
AFDC Caseloads in Massachusetts by Year and Rate of Change: 1960–1981

|  | 1960 | 1970 | 1977 | 1978 | 1979 | 1980 | 1981* |
|---|---|---|---|---|---|---|---|
| AFDC Cases | 15,000 | 62,600 | 119,115 | 121,727 | 119,954 | 121,057 | 120,764 |
| Rate of Change |  | +317% | +90% | +2% | −1% | +0.9% | −0.2% |

Sources: HEW Public Assistance Statistics, MDPW Caseload Reports
* The 1981 figures indicates the initial impact of changes made under the Omnibus Budget
 Reconciliation Act of 1981.

spond to its own error rate crisis, it would have to produce results in Massachusetts and other large, high error states, although it had little control over their day-to-day administrative practices.

Through quality control and the threat of fiscal sanctions, HEW exerted a powerful influence on the timing and the character of state welfare reform. Although it would be unfair to say that the state's interest in reform was externally motivated, that interest had been insufficient in past years to surmount numerous political and implementation obstacles. The error rate crisis provided an immediate impetus for reform and created the sense of urgency necessary to achieve it. In addition to its timing, the character of state welfare reform reflected the influence of federal quality control. This influence was indirect, occurring as state reformers referred to quality control to define their problems and measure their progress. Although the state sustained the appearance of autonomy in the design and implementation of administrative welfare reform, it is important to explore how the volition of state officials was constrained and their choices bounded by HEW's indirect influence on their perceived interests and, thus, the value placed on alternative courses of action.[1]

## The Environment for Reform

Paradoxically, federal quality control requirements had been in place since 1973, but more than five years later the MDPW could point to few advances in reducing its error rate. Error-reducing initiatives considered over this time tended to move forward slowly, if at all. Despite the promise of the state's "corrective action" reports to HEW, few major reforms had actually been implemented prior to 1979. What changed in 1979 to make error rate reduction management's number one priority?

The most obvious influence on the state's interest calculus was the prospect of $9.1 million in fiscal penalties following the reinstatement of sanctions provisions by HEW. However, this did not fully explain the intensity with which the state mounted a virtual "war on error" commencing in the spring of 1979. Despite the potential cost of ignoring the error rate, state attention could have been deflected by other issues, possibly involving even greater costs or benefits. Or, if the thrust of federal interests conflicted with intensely held state interests, state energy could have been applied to resisting HEW pressure, either overtly or through more subtle "coping mechanisms." For example, before 1979, the state's primary response to HEW's highly touted Six State Strategy had been to develop elaborate "corrective action plans," which promised on paper to combat errors in a variety of ways. But, as noted, only a few relatively minor initiatives actually were implemented during this period.

However, by 1979, the environment for reform had changed in several important respects. First, in contrast to previous years, there were no issues of a magnitude comparable to the error rate crisis to compete for management's attention.[2] Second, HEW's interest in tightening up the welfare system was compatible with the political agenda of the new governor of Massachusetts, Edward J. King, who assumed office in January 1979. In his campaign, King had pursued a hard line against "welfare chiselers" and promised to cut welfare spending by $250 million. Given his pledge to cut spending and his anti-welfare image, King could hardly welcome the imposition of millions of dollars in fiscal sanctions because of poor welfare management. Third, just as King and his new welfare commissioner, John D. Pratt Jr., entered office, HEW descended on the new administration with the unmistakable message that the current sanctions threat was a serious one and, moreover, things might soon be worse if Congressman Michel succeeded in tightening sanctions policy.

For the new commissioner, the error rate crisis assumed overwhelming importance. To begin with, the error rate was clearly the measure against which his administration would be judged by the governor and others. But, in addition, Pratt saw in the crisis an opportunity to implement a broad reform program, an objective that had been out of reach of his predecessors. A Harvard Business School graduate and finance official in two prior state administrations, Pratt was a professional manager and regarded himself as a social welfare advocate. Recalling his views upon his appointment as commissioner, he described himself as being excited by the challenge of transforming a poorly managed and much maligned welfare bureaucracy into a modern and efficient claims processing agency (interview, 1981). From Pratt's perspective, as he explained it, reform would not only save tax dollars but also would restore legitimacy to the welfare system and improve service delivery to the poor. He contended that efforts to liberalize benefits and expand services would fail to win support until the public was satisfied that tax dollars were not being squandered by a wasteful, sloppy bureaucracy. Writing in 1981, Pratt asserted that "one effect of poor administration is distracted public attention. Fundamental policy issues surrounding a particular need in society become overshadowed by poor organizational performance. . . . Accusations of 'recipient fraud' and 'employee incompetence' cast a shadow over effective policy development" (Pratt, 1981, p. 22). Pratt's assessment of his policy options was strikingly similar to the assessments HEW secretaries Califano and Harris had made at the federal level.

## Developing an Administrative Strategy

The two-year reform effort launched by Commissioner Pratt in the spring of 1979 constituted a virtual "war on error" in Massachusetts. It also initiated a long overdue adminsitrative assault on a public agency that embodied many of the worst features of the archetypical welfare bureaucracy. The critical task facing reformers was to devise and implement initiatives that would penetrate a decentralized, street-level bureaucracy and affect the routine decisionmaking of hundreds of lower-level workers so that they produced fewer quality control errors. In several respects to be briefly outlined, this was a particularly formidable task.

First, management control was made highly problematic by an organizational structure that was decentralized, with authority divided among regional and local offices that were nearly feudal in their operating autonomy. Second, the bureaucracy was heavily populated by social workers who were accustomed to exercising discretion according to the role expectations and norms of the social work profession. This social work orientation had contributed to the perception that they were too liberal in distributing benefits.

Third, over the years, bureaucrats had established patterns of behavior and practice that enabled them to cope with demands—from above and below—in their work environment. An entrenched bureaucracy and its established organizational pathways and norms are not readily changed from above.[3] Finally, discretion was an intrinsic component of the production of welfare policy at the street level. Workers necessarily made judgments about individual needs and the applicability of complicated welfare regulations in determining eligibility for benefits. Standardization could be increased, but only at the cost of diminishing the tailoring of benefits to fit individual circumstances.

Given its reform objectives, how could management turn the attention of the welfare bureaucracy to error reduction—and quickly? How could the production process be reorganized to maximize the attributes of bureaucratic performance monitored by quality control? How could the welfare bureaucracy be made accountable for the "quality" of its work, as the state was accountable to HEW?

In management's pursuit of administrative reform, quality control served as a guide, model, and measure. The MDPW relied heavily on data developed in accordance with federal quality control requirements to identify and evaluate administrative problems. Those data, which measured some 45 elements of payment accuracy, enabled analysts to specify the types, seriousness, and causes of the department's payment errors. MDPW and HEW analysts also used these data to rank errors according to their cost, measured in terms of potential fiscal sanctions, providing an obvious strategic guide for reformers seeking to minimize the department's error rate.

These analyses pointed to two broad categories of problems. First, more than half of the state's error rate could be attributed generally to worker sloppiness and failure to process paperwork according to department rules. For example, failures to record recipient social security numbers—so-called enumeration errors—were estimated to account for nearly one-third of the department's 24.8 percent error rate for the period ending March 1979. In addition, worker failure to use information that was available in case records was estimated to account for up to 40 percent of the error rate, cutting across specific error types.[4]

The second major category of errors occurred as workers exercised discretion in determining eligibility and benefit levels. Judgments concerning how far to probe into applicant eligibility, the acceptability of evidence, and the interpretation of complex and ambiguous policies resulted in errors when they differed from the judgments of quality control reviewers. The components of such errors were less clear than in the case of specific procedural mistakes.

However, using quality control data, department analysts were able to make inferences about the attributes of erroneous judgments. For example, WIN errors, errors that occurred when benefits were paid to recipients who had not registered for the state's mandatory work training program (WIN), were among the five "most costly" payment errors in terms of potential fiscal sanctions. According to quality control analyses, at least one-third of these errors occurred because workers failed to make appropriate judgments about medical exemptions from the registration requirement. The components of this error included the failure to verify the grounds for a medical exemption adequately and the incorrect application of policy requirements (Massachusetts Department of Public Welfare, Jan. 21, 1980).

Management's reform strategy addressed these two broad dimensions of the error rate problem. Initially, management directed its efforts toward the short-term objective of cleaning up specific errors, many procedural, which were among the most costly in terms of fiscal sanctions. Not only were these errors relatively easy to identify and correct on an ad hoc basis, but a "quick fix" would produce an immediate and visible impact on the state's error rate.

Over the long term, however, management recognized that its performance objectives could be achieved and sustained only by institutionalizing a "highly structured and controlled system of normal practice," as one high-level official put it (interview, 1981). This dimension of administrative reform was far more complex and problematic, involving the assertion of management influence over the exercise of worker discretion. In recasting the welfare production process to minimize the error rate, management proceeded to translate quality control standards into procedural rules that limited worker discretion. In addition, it introduced accountability for procedural compliance by developing an internal monitoring system modeled on federal quality control. Several of management's most intense and far-reaching initiatives to reduce the error rate and reform the welfare bureaucracy are examined in the sections that follow.

# Phase One: Special Projects

The quality control results for the review period ending in March 1979 were dismal. The error rate had jumped more than nine percentage points above the previous period. Worse still, this surge occurred just as the new sanctions regulations were being put into effect, making Massachusetts liable for some $9 million in fiscal penalties.

Analyses indicated that this apparent deterioration in administrative performance was almost entirely an artifact of a change in quality control measurement. For the first time, federal reviewers had counted in error any payment made to a recipient who was not identified in case records by a social security number. Congress had made "enumeration" by social security number a condition of categorical eligibility for AFDC in 1976.[5] In 1978, HEW notified states that quality control would subsequently deem erroneous any payment made to an unenumerated recipient, more specifically, any recipient whose social security number was not accurately recorded in the case record.

Massachusetts officials argued, as did officials from other states, that the failure to enumerate recipients constituted only a "paper error," one that when corrected did not alter the payment to which an individual was entitled. They reasoned that these errors should be excluded from the error rate used as the basis for fiscal sanctions and that sanctions based on enumeration errors could be overturned in court. Even after it became clear that HEW would include these errors in the error rate, the MDPW made only a limited effort to enforce the enumeration requirement prior to the error rate "crisis" in 1979.

## The Enumeration Blitz

Without a major effort, it was obvious that a substantial portion of the department's caseload would continue to be out of compliance with this requirement. The reason was that the enumeration requirement exemplified precisely that type of procedural obligation that workers tended to ignore or overlook.[6] It appeared to many to be irrelevant to substantive eligibility; the enumeration process could be time-consuming, and there were multiple opportunities to miss steps along the way.

The process required workers to give unenumerated applicants or recipients a form that they were to take to the local Social Security (SSA) office to apply for a number. At the local SSA office, applicants were required to verify their identity by obtaining and providing documentation of residence, age, and identity. Some weeks or months later, SSA would send a social security card to the applicant, who was then responsible for bringing it to the welfare office, where the number would be recorded.

There were two components to the enumeration problem. First, an unknown number of recipients had complied with application procedures but had never received a social security card, or if they had, the number had not been recorded in their case files. The MDPW had begun to address this problem in 1978, developing a computer link to the SSA that would automatically feed social security numbers directly to the MDPW. In addition, the MDPW was installing a system to alert workers to cases in which no number had been received after 90 days.

However, these actions did not remedy the most serious problem. The department estimated that more than 45,000 dependents among the state's 350,000 AFDC recipients were unenumerated. It was this backlog that accounted for most of the rise in the state's error rate when enumeration errors were incorporated into the quality control review.

When the 24.8 percent March error rate was published, one official later recalled, "There was yelling and screaming. People who never cared about numbers were talking error rate and error rate" (interview, 1981). Suddenly, enumeration errors were propelled to the top of management's error "hit list." A special enumeration project, launched in a barrage of memos and meetings in December 1979, targeted these 45,000 unenumerated dependents. Its aims were to ensure that a social security number was recorded for each recipient and to terminate benefits to those who failed to verify that they had complied with application requirements. The project lasted nearly four months and involved overtime for hundreds of workers.

Recipients, whose names appeared on special computer printouts, were notified by mail and later instructed by telephone to come to the welfare office, bringing their social security cards, if they had them. Those who could not provide cards were told to apply for them at the Boston SSA office. They were given the department's new ENUM-2 form, to be signed at the SSA and returned to the welfare office verifying that the application process had been completed. Recipients who had previously applied for numbers and did not have an ENUM-2—even those who could produce an earlier version of the ENUM-2 as verification—were required to reapply. Under an agreement negotiated with federal quality control officials, the MDPW would receive a 90–day grace period before an unenumerated case was counted in error, but only if the file contained a completed ENUM-2 form.

Hundreds of recipients, responding to MDPW notices, clogged local offices. Workers were extended beyond capacity, despite temporarily neglecting other duties. Long waiting lines, common in the larger offices, were repeated at the SSA office. Many applicants, who were unaware of SSA's verification requirements, had to make several trips in order to complete the application process.

Welfare workers were assigned weekly enumeration quotas to be met by voluntary overtime. Pressed to meet their quotas, workers had little time to assist recipients in the sometimes difficult application process. Requests for other types of assistance were postponed or ignored in the midst of the administratively generated enumeration crisis. However, this massive disruption of office routine was regarded by MDPW management as a small price to pay for substantially improving the error rate. Furthermore, as one official explained, management viewed local office routine as so poor that the disruption could not make it much worse.

Management closely followed the progress of the enumeration project, requiring weekly reports from each local office. Numbers of cases corrected and those remaining were centrally tabulated and local office ratings distributed throughout the department. Directors were placed on notice that they would be held accountable for office performance. Those whose offices failed to achieve enumeration quotas during the four-month campaign and continued to have large numbers of enumeration errors were threatened with demotion or dismissal. Subsequently, in a move that was felt throughout the department, the commissioner placed 16 directors on probation.

As intended, the enumeration project had the direct effect of virtually eliminating the backlog of unenumerated cases. Between the start of the project in December 1979 and its conclusion in March 1980, the social security number error rate was cut from 8.2 percent to 2.4 percent.[7] Contributing to management's ability to achieve such impressive results was the one-to-one correlation between enumeration errors and quality control errors—correcting one eliminated the possibility of the other. Also, ironically, the MDPW's earlier disregard of the enumeration requirement had produced a large bulge in the error rate that was relatively easy to eliminate. In these respects, the enumeration problem differed from other administrative errors which tended to be more difficult to target and were more deeply ingrained in the welfare delivery system.

### Making the Transition: Operation Perform

Management moved to consolidate and extend its gains in reducing the error rate with a second and more ambitious project. Operation Perform (an acronym for Payment Error Reduction through Field Operations Revisions and Maintenance) combined the short- and long-term objectives of management's reform program. Beginning with the eight largest offices, Operation Perform included a one-shot correction of case records, followed by a reorganization of record-keeping systems and establishment of rules of practice and monitoring systems that would insure the records were accurately maintained. Management's publicly stated goal was the achievement of a 13 percent error rate for the September 1980 quality control review period (MDPW news release, June 1979).

Promoted with a great deal of flash and publicity in the summer of 1980, Operation Perform moved strongly on the heels of the enumeration campaign to impress on the welfare bureaucracy the importance of reducing the error rate. The groundwork for this effort had been laid in February in a three-day Conference on Critical Management Strategies for Error Elimination, attended by regional managers, office directors, and their assistants. At the conference, Commissioner Pratt had outlined a broad set of agency goals and explained that the department's high error rate indicated that those broad goals were not being met.

As in other elements of management's reform program, this project was formulated on the basis of quality control data. Quality control analysts estimated that as much as 40 percent of payment errors could be blamed on sloppy record-keeping practices, which made it difficult for workers to locate and act on available information. For example, one analysis estimated that 31 percent of payment errors involving earned income cases could have been avoided if workers had acted on information available in the case record.

It is not difficult to understand how information could be lost in case files, which at times covered 5 to 10 years (or longer) and could grow to be several inches thick. Documents of temporary interest, such as letters from recipients, old rent receipts, and social worker commentaries, were interspersed with documents needed as part of the permanent record, such as social security cards, birth certificates, and marriage licenses. As cases were periodically transferred to workers unfamiliar with family history, the document trail simultaneously became more important yet more difficult to capture.

In dealing with this problem, the first phase of Operation Perform adopted an approach similar to that employed in the enumeration project. But, instead of one quality control error (enumeration), this project targeted a variety of documentation errors that were associated with quality control errors. Using a case review guide, which specified documents to be included in each AFDC case record, workers were to review and correct deficiencies in each of their case files. For example, workers were to check for copies of birth or baptismal certificates to verify grantee ages and relationships, school attendance verification letters for children over age 16 exempted from WIN registration, and five consecutive wage stubs for grantees with earnings.

In at least one instance, the specifications for the case review guide were narrower than the department's own policy. In Operation Perform, forms verifying WIN registration were accepted only if less than one year old, whereas department regulations set no time limit on the validity of a recipient's registration documentation. In the process of "correcting" their records, workers required recipients who had registered earlier to re-register. After corrections were made, workers were to reorganize case records according to a standard format. This would enable workers and reviewers to match records quickly against a checklist indicating required documentation and processing.

As a by-product of this correction process, as in the case of the enumeration project, recipients were sent from office to crowded office to comply with new procedural requirements. Also, as in the previous campaign, workers were pulled from other duties to meet quotas for case review and correction (120 cases per month). Given the administrative burden imposed by this project, it is not surprising that offices with limited resources would cope with these demands by rationing public access to caseworkers. In at least one large office, for several months workers were unavailable to applicants or recipients until 11:15 each morning, and for the remainder of the day, only a single "duty worker" was expected to field all inquiries and problems for each four-person unit.[8]

Two major bottlenecks extended for much longer than anticipated the period during which Operation Perform disrupted local office routine. The first bottleneck occurred when replacement case file folders, into which reorganized records were to be moved, turned out to be too flimsy and new supplies had to be ordered. However, the backlog that most troubled local offices occurred in the review process itself.

The central office had sent special teams of Operation Perform reviewers to check the accuracy of files corrected by caseworkers (a "mini" quality control review). These teams were composed of former social workers, those regarded as least qualified to fill positions in the newly formed Department of Social Services and, thus, left in an uncertain status at the MDPW. Although they received special training for this project, many of the reviewers had little expertise or recent experience in processing AFDC payments.

In a central office survey of two of these teams, one-quarter to one-half of their reviews were determined to be incorrect. Reviewers both were sending accurate cases back to workers for further "correction" and were overlooking worker errors that the central office intended to correct.[9] To compensate, local office supervisors had begun to recheck, rather than sample, each case received as completed, that is, following the second set of worker corrections. Given this cumbersome process, the director of one large office estimated that it would take, not three months as anticipated, but close to a year to complete the correction and reorganization process.

For these and other reasons, the grandiose ambitions of Operation Perform were largely unrealized and the project abandoned after the initial review and reorganization were completed. Nevertheless, with this project, the department pushed forward the process of standardizing case processing and developing methods to monitor and hold lower-level workers accountable for quality control errors. On the one hand, these special projects antagonized and confused local office workers because of inconsistent applications of policy and the frantic pace of work required. On the other hand, workers could not doubt that management was serious about reducing the error rate. The message that "error is everything" had begun to penetrate the welfare bureaucracy.

## Phase Two: Recasting the Production Routine

The "blitzkrieg" of special projects was viewed as only an interim measure. In the second phase of administrative reform, management turned toward its long-term objective of recasting the production routine so that workers' benefits decisions, as well as their paperwork, would conform to quality control standards. However, unlike enumeration and record-keeping failures, the problem of worker discretion was not easily divided into discrete components for which corrective strategies could be formulated. In practice, addressing this problem meant dealing with some of the most difficult aspects of welfare work.

For one thing, worker discretion was necessary to apply broad and complex welfare policies to fit individual needs and circumstances. As Mills explains:

> The decision logic that the caseworker must execute is often very complicated. Inexperience and the lack of training may lead to confusion as to appropriate policy interpretations. In seeking to prescribe action in all conceivable circumstances, policy manuals become unwieldy. Rules change frequently, and ... caseworkers are unable to keep pace. The stated policy provisions may be ambiguous or even contradictory, and it is only conventional practice that establishes right from wrong. ... *The essential judgment—e.g., whether the basis of financial needs makes the family categorically eligible for assistance, what constitutes countable income and assets—must be made by individual workers exercising substantial discretion.* (Mills, 1981, p. 25; emphasis added)

Second, there was a tension between this "necessary" discretion and management's interest in standardizing decisions to reduce the variability associated with payment errors and inequities in client treatment. Third, even if management were willing to trade individual fit for decisionmaking consistency, then enforcing worker conformity with processing rules would be problematic. As Lipsky explains, the problem of enforcement in a street-level bureaucracy occurs in part because of "the conflict between the objectives and orientations of street-level bureaucrats and those in higher authority roles." Furthermore, welfare workers were capable of resisting efforts to curb their autonomy (Lipsky, 1980, esp. chs. 1–2). How were reformers to approach these problems of worker discretion?

### Providing Information

From management's perspective, the ideal worker was one who would make benefits decisions that did not produce quality control errors. Without adequate information, workers could not be expected to produce decisions that were "accurate" by quality control standards. To the extent that department policies were not known or understood and the practices that would implement them unspecified and uncertain, the MDPW provided far less than an ideal environment for accurate decisionmaking.

Although policy changed continuously, the department had no effective system for making current regulations accessible to its workers. Moreover, formal policy did not deal with the variety of circumstances presented to workers and, at times, regulations were vague or inconsistent. Compounding these problems, the department lacked a clear set of procedures that, if followed, would correctly implement its policies. New workers did not receive adequate training according to a set of standard principles or practices and often learned piecemeal on the job.

These deficiencies were quickly apparent to the Pratt administration, which took several simple steps to remedy them. First, the department recodified AFDC policies in a new manual, which was distributed to each welfare worker in a looseleaf binder. The manual's pages could be replaced by workers as they became obsolete. Second, the department prepared its first worker handbook, which detailed the steps to be taken in processing welfare grants and other related benefits. Third, the department initiated training programs, which disseminated and interpreted formal policy according to a consistent standard of practice and stressed the importance of avoiding quality control errors.

On their face, management initiatives to inform and train its workforce were straightforward. Through a variety of methods, workers were generally informed of what they were to do and how they were to do it. However, in the process of specifying policies and procedures, management also began to reduce the scope of worker discretion and limit the range of decision options. For example, department regulations did not uniformly require proof of residence (CMR 303.400b). The manual stated that "*if verification of residence is necessary*, the method of verification depends on the residency requirement the applicant or recipient claims to have met" (emphasis added). Eight types of proof were listed, including a signed statement from the landlord; a deed; postal, church, utility, employment or voter registration records; and auto license or registration.

However, the handbook further specified and narrowed department requirements, stating that "the fact that the applicant or recipient actually lives in the Commonwealth *must* be verified." It then listed five acceptable proofs, including a rent receipt or lease, a signed statement from a landlord, post office or utility records, and a deed (sec. 4040). In practice, verification of residence could be troublesome for recipients who shared housing and were not listed on rental or utility records. Consequently, changing the verification requirements to narrow the parameters of worker discretion made it more difficult for some applicants to prove their eligibility.

Of course, the policies and practices disseminated to workers through the manual, handbook, and training were not exclusively concerned with quality control errors. Nor were such errors the exclusive concern of welfare workers, who each day had to cope with multiple and sometimes overwhelming demands from above and below. Management's specification of its demands and general instruction on how to meet them were necessary but insufficient to assert central control over the production process for several reasons.

Workers were caught in a crossfire of pressing needs—among them those of applicants for assistance, their own for job satisfaction, and management's for production. Not infrequently, satisfaction of competing demands was a "zero sum" proposition. Why, then, should workers choose to comply with requirements of policy and practice that were specified by management? Given limited organizational resources and multiple demands, it would be rational for workers to ignore procedural requirements that were difficult or time-consuming or were likely to strain relations with their clients. Moreover, bureaucrats who regarded themselves as social workers could be expected to place perceived client needs ahead of formal administrative requirements in deciding how to respond to requests for assistance. One would also expect them informally to resist restrictions on their discretion that threatened their autonomy and status.

In sum, having asserted its demands and addressed the information problem, management still confronted two related problems. First, there was a certain amount of "irreducible" discretion in welfare work, and the complexity of welfare policy limited management's ability to fully specify enforceable procedural rules. Second, even for those elements of decision-making that could be specified, worker compliance could not necessarily be enforced.

## Reducing Discretion

Administrative reformers would have to address these dimensions of worker discretion if their procedural specifications were to be translated from paper to practice. Federal quality control suggested a model approach for state reformers. Through performance measurement, street-level bureaucrats could be made accountable for complying with selected management requirements, much as states were accountable to HEW for meeting quality control requirements. Worker compliance could be enforced by imposing penalties based on performance scores.

The Pratt administration responded to the error rate crisis by transforming a little-used department monitoring system into a relatively sophisticated instrument designed to hold local office workers accountable for observing selected processing rules.[10] The MDPW's quality assurance system, as it existed up to that time, had provided only a crude measure of worker productivity. It represented the type of limited effort previous administrations had made to address the long-festering error rate problem.

*Early Efforts.* For example, in response to quality control analyses that indicated that payment errors could be reduced if cases were more frequently redetermined, the MDPW in 1978 had established worker redetermination quotas. (In redetermining eligibility, benefits are adjusted to account for changes in family circumstances.) Workers who failed to achieve their quotas were placed on corrective action. Under this form of probation, their daily tasks were closely monitored, they were confined to the office and prohibited from making home visits,[11] and they were unable to receive promotions. Unless sufficient improvements were made, they could be demoted or dismissed.

As workers sought to maximize performance on this measure, redetermination productivity did, in fact, increase. But workers tended to improve their productivity by selecting the least complicated cases to redetermine and, then, redetermining them frequently. Since these were also the cases least likely to involve quality control errors, management found it necessary to devise a counterstrategy to meet its objectives.

The MDPW next established a "priority redetermination" system, which required workers to meet their quotas by redetermining selected cases specified by management in descending order of priority. Cases received priority if they had characteristics that, according to quality control analyses, made them error-prone. Error-prone characteristics included, for example, the length of time since the previous redetermination, presence of earned income, dependents in certain age groups, and claimed income deductibles. Also among the priority cases were those in which fraud was suspected based on a comparison of MDPW case records and employer wage records compiled by the state Department of Revenue. Again, management was confounded. Pressures to meet quotas and deal with the most difficult cases were counterproductive to management's interest in improving payment accuracy, because they created incentives to sacrifice quality for quantity in case processing.

What was needed was an accountability instrument that, in effect, could bring federal quality control to the local office bureaucracy. The development of such an instrument was necessary because the federal quality control review sampled only enough cases to measure performance at the state level. Expanding the sample size to achieve statistical validity at the local office level was far too costly in time and personnel. (A quality control reviewer conducted a full field investigation of recipient eligibility, completing on average only about 10 investigations per month.) A less costly alternative was to devise a performance measure that could be produced through a relatively simple desk review of selected case files.

*A New System.* HEW assisted the department in transforming quality assurance into such a system, supporting an MDPW study of its most costly administrative errors (in terms of fiscal sanctions) and the procedural steps that could minimize the commission of these errors.[12] In addition, in mid-1979 HEW "loaned" the state its top quality control expert from the Boston regional office to supervise the MDPW's newly intensified effort to develop and implement quality assurance as an office-level monitoring system.

The new quality assurance system was introduced state-wide in March 1980 after being tested in the state's 20 largest offices. It produced office performance scores that combined case accuracy (measured as the percentage of cases error-free) and compliance with productivity quotas. It addressed the imbalance of previous measures by giving three times the weight to accuracy as to productivity. Based on quarterly reviews of 80 percent of the redeterminations conducted in each welfare office, quality assurance produced statistically valid scores for each local office supervisory unit. Unlike quality control, which drew its sample from all active cases, quality assurance monitored only redeterminations.

Using a standard review guide, quality assurance teams could check case records for procedural errors that were associated with quality control errors. Such errors did not necessarily indicate that an overpayment or payment to an ineligible person (that is, a quality control error) had occurred, nor did reviewers independently investigate recipient eligibility. Quality assurance monitored only whether workers complied with procedural rules for investigating recipient claims and whether procedures were carried out consistently and accurately.

Despite the differences between federal quality control and state quality assurance, the influence of the federal measure on the design of the state's monitoring system was straightforward. Quite simply, quality assurance specified attributes of local office performance in terms of procedural steps designed to prevent the commission of the MDPW's most costly quality control errors, involving enumeration, school attendance, relationship of grantees, earned income, bank deposits, and unearned income.[13]

***The "Prudent Standard."*** In the process of monitoring procedural compliance, quality assurance also specified attributes of what the MDPW termed a "prudent standard" of practice. The prudent standard was procedurally rigorous in requiring claimants to prove their eligibility for benefits. It effectively reversed the "declaration standard," which assumed the veracity of a claimant's statements unless there was a reason for doubt.[14] Under the terms of the MDPW's prudent standard, claimants were routinely required to verify up to 30 aspects of eligibility (for example, age, school attendance, residence, bank accounts). In addition, worker discretion was reduced by limiting the types of documentary evidence that they could accept.

In a few instances, verification requirements specified by quality assurance were identical to quality control requirements. For example, both required as evidence of enumeration that case files contain either a signed ENUM-2 application form or a copy of a social security card and that the numbers be correctly transcribed into the case record. However, for the most part, quality assurance targeted procedural rules that were intended to reduce the probability that workers would overpay grantees or make payments to ineligible persons. In effect, quality assurance transformed the attributes of case accuracy monitored by quality control into procedural requirements that could be enforced at the local office level.

For example, quality assurance reviewed case records for copies of recipients' birth certificates or other specified documentation of parent-child relationship and birth date. Worker failure to obtain acceptable verification of birth and relationship was regarded as a quality assurance error. But the absence of these documents did not necessarily mean that recipients were ineligible for benefits. Nor, therefore, did it necessarily result in a quality control error—that is, an overpayment or payment to an ineligible person.

Similarly, quality assurance sought to minimize the probability of quality control errors, such as those involving excess assets, failure to register for WIN, earned income discrepancies, and incorrect benefit calculations. It did this by checking to see that workers (1) obtained verification of bank balances dated within 45 days of the redetermination; (2) correctly followed procedures for determining whether work registration was required (for example, that workers obtained verification that children over age 16 were attending school and were therefore exempt); (3) verified WIN registration, if mandatory, by supplying a copy of the registration form; (4) obtained five consecutive wage stubs dated within six weeks of the home visit and correctly used them in calculating earned income and deductions (and also obtained proof of claimed work-related expenses); and (5) correctly applied formulas for calculating benefits.

**The Informal System.** Through formal measures, such as quality assurance, the policy manual, the worker handbook, and training programs, management increasingly specified and standardized procedural rules and held workers accountable for complying with them. Nevertheless, worker discretion continued to be an intrinsic component of the benefits determination process, necessary to reconcile complex and ambiguous regulations with an infinite configuration of family circumstances. Informally, as particular issues came to the attention of quality assurance reviewers, they filled policy gaps and extended the interpretation of procedural rules to cover additional aspects of case processing.

In effect, local office administrators received continuing instruction in acceptable practice through routine conferences with the quality assurance reviewers who visited their offices. Caseworkers learned how quality assurance wanted them to interpret policy as their cases were returned to them for error correction. Occasionally, administrators, trying to minimize their offices' error scores, questioned or challenged reviewer decisions, particularly when regulations were unclear. In responding to questions, reviewers adapted and clarified regulations and specified the practices local offices were required to follow.

A reported encounter between a reviewer and office administrator illustrates how this process worked.[15] In this instance, the administrator challenged a quality assurance finding that a case was in error because the worker had failed to require dependent children to apply for social security death benefits. The administrator pointed out that case records indicated that the deceased was not legally the children's father. Therefore, it was pointless to insist that the children seek death benefits for which they did not qualify. The quality assurance reviewer refused to consider whether the worker's judgment was accurate or reasonable, asserting that the worker had erred simply in exercising discretion rather than observing procedural rules. He told the administrator, "You have to go through all the steps."[16]

Such decisions were rarely appealed. As one official closely involved in the implementation of the quality assurance system explained, the reviewers tended to be the only central office figures to visit local offices regularly. "We're the only people of authority they see. They ask a question and our supervisors respond, and that's the word of God." He added that there was little reluctance to assume this role: "When someone asks, we'll give them an opinion" (interview, 1982).

On occasion, this process created a reverse policy flow, and the monitors of policy implementation became, in effect, the policymakers. For example, the policy manual specified that certain verifications must be "current." However, quality assurance, according to one official, "needed some objective standard" by which to judge currentness and settled on a 45–day rule. Subsequently, the department's regulations were revised to require that certain verifications be dated within 45 days of the eligibility determination. As this official put it, "They changed the policy to go along with the way we've been interpreting it all along" (interview, 1982).

**Local Office Accountability.** Quality assurance not only specified the procedural attributes of accurate casework and measured office performance but also provided a basis on which management could hold welfare bureaucrats accountable for performance. Quality assurance enabled management to reach directly to local office directors, who were subject to demotion or dismissal (and at minimum considerable pressure) on the basis of their performance scores. Regional managers were required to place directors on corrective action (a probationary status) if their quality assurance error rates exceeded 10 percent for more than three quarters. Demotion could follow unless improvement were demonstrated within a specified period (unpub. MDPW memo, Nov. 1979).

In the case of one large Boston office, which consistently scored among the bottom tenth percentile of all offices, the central office sent its own small, high-level team to evaluate local problems and oversee their correction. Essentially, central office staff temporarily usurped the director's authority. More than one year later, administrative staff in the local office said they felt as though higher-ups were continually looking over their shoulders and that they were "walking on eggs" (interview, 1981).

In a sense, the performance that counted most was that of street-level workers who were farthest removed from direct central office pressure and control. Quality assurance figures were not statistically valid at the worker level. Moreover, the department continued to penalize workers for failing to meet redetermination quotas but did not invoke similar penalties for inaccurate case processing. Under these circumstances, one would expect workers to continue to trade accuracy for quantity.

In practice, however, quality assurance did reach to the street-level worker via a somewhat byzantine path. Supervisors, who were accountable for errors made by their units, became increasingly cautious about "signing off" redeterminations that were submitted to them as completed. Seeking to minimize quality assurance errors, they refused to sign redeterminations if they had doubts about whether workers properly observed procedural rules, particularly whether workers adequately documented proof of eligibility. Without these signatures, workers would not receive credit toward their redetermination quotas. This placed caseworkers trying to meet productivity quotas in a bind. In order to avoid delays in reaching their quotas, workers learned to be zealous—even excessively so—in observing procedural rules.

### Extending Management Authority

The preceding accountability measures enabled management to penetrate the welfare bureaucracy and begin to redirect local office routine. Under the rubric of error rate reduction, management took further steps to centralize and reinforce its authority. These steps were aimed at removing or reducing the power of bureaucrats whose interests and orientations ran counter to the thrust of management's reform program.[17]

Rather than fight over issues of discretion and proceduralism, management sought to replace workers oriented toward the norms of the social work profession with others who would be comfortable as claims processors. In 1979, the MDPW created a new civil service position called Financial Assistance Worker (FAW), which formally redefined as clerical the job of local office caseworkers. Instead of needing an advanced degree in social work, FAWs were required to have only a high school diploma and two years of experience in a human services organization. In recruiting and training new workers, the MDPW emphasized the clerical nature of the job. As one official explained, "We didn't want to get a bunch of frustrated social workers" (interview 1981). Given rapid employee turnover, such a change in recruitment and hiring could begin to alter the character of the bureaucracy relatively quickly.

The Service Employees International Union (SEIU), which represented welfare workers, proved to be a relatively weak opponent of de-professionalization. This may largely be due to its preoccupation at that time with organizing the new Department of Social Services, to which the social workers who formed the base of the union's membership had been transferred. Officials in the top echelon of the department claim that they kept de-professionalization from becoming a controversial issue by emphasizing their efforts to support welfare workers and relieve them of the more tedious elements of the job by routinizing and simplifying procedures.

Management faced tougher adversaries in its efforts to assert control over the middle-level bureaucracy, which stood between the central and local offices. Regional office managers who could provide patronage to area legislators through local office appointment powers sustained something of an independent political base and, thus, substantial autonomy from central office control. According to department insiders, they had mobilized outside support to block efforts to eliminate regional offices.

Using the rhetoric of "good management" and the threat of quality control sanctions, Pratt reportedly convinced key legislative leaders that a centrally administered merit system was needed to provide career ladders that would keep competent people in the department—a prerequisite for reducing the error rate. Given the political delicacy of these transactions, details are difficult to verify. Nevertheless, Pratt did wrest from the regional offices the authority to appoint local office directors. He then took further steps to break up the patronage network by requiring directors to go outside the local office to fill at least 75 percent of their administrative slots. Although observers have varying judgments, those closest to the commissioner's office believe Pratt may have consumed valuable political resources in taking on the regional office-legislative alliance. The enemies made in this battle and the commissioner's continuing resistance to patronage demands are generally thought to have caused his resignation after only 18 months in office, despite his success in reducing the error rate.[18]

## Reform Reconsidered

Within a short time, the error rate crisis was translated into a far-reaching program of state-level administrative welfare reform. Although state officials operated relatively free of federal intrusion in developing and implementing their program, the attributes of performance they sought to maximize were those that HEW measured through its quality control system. In the drive to reform welfare administration, management's attention was directed almost exclusively to those attributes of performance that were subject to federal sanctions.

Accountability measures disregarded departmental regulations and procedures intended to make benefits accessible to the needy and to tailor them to individual needs. This included regulations that

- made workers responsible for assisting recipients who had problems in obtaining required verifications;
- permitted recipients to receive extensions when unable to meet deadlines for providing verifications;
- required workers to inform recipients fully of the range of benefits to which they were entitled;
- established time standards for workers to update case records to in-

dicate changes that would increase AFDC benefits (such as the birth of a baby); and

- permitted recipients in certain instances to provide verifications other than those preferred by the department.[19]

There is little evidence to suggest that, in the process of reform, officials seriously considered the tradeoffs made between consideration of individual needs and mass processing, between worker professionalism and de-professionalization. Nor does the record suggest concern for the implications of the shift from a standard of presumptive eligibility to a standard requiring detailed proof of eligibility. It is significant, on its face, that such inherently political decisions were largely non-decisions, the preferred direction of tradeoffs essentially presumed, during the process of reforming the state's welfare system. In obscuring the political dimensions of administrative reform, while establishing a structure that heavily biased its thrust, federal quality control had an indirect influence on state welfare reform that was profound.

# 6

# The Consequences of Reform

The Massachusetts reform campaign was a manifest success. According to Commissioner Pratt, reform's success could be measured in terms of its net result—the state's error rate declined almost 67 percent from its high of 24.8 percent in 1979 to 8.2 percent by 1981. Touting the success of administrative reform under his leadership, Pratt drew optimistic lessons for other public managers. He asserted that his experience demonstrated that "state agencies can be managed," but not by merely "tinkering at the top." Rather, he explained, reform's success depended on "fundamental change penetrating each local welfare office" (Pratt, 1981, p. 2).

But, significantly, neither state nor federal reformers seriously questioned the meaning of that achievement or whether "fundamental change" in the welfare delivery system might have effects beyond those measured by quality control. It is time to address these questions.

## The Measure of Management's Success

At minimum, one might reasonably infer from the decline in the state's error rate that fewer excess payments were made. However, the extent of even this "improvement" remains uncertain. To begin with, more than half (about nine percentage points) of the state's error rate reduction of 16.6 percentage points occurred through the correction of WIN and enumeration errors. Yet, when corrected, these "paper errors" did not necessarily alter the distribution of welfare payments or save taxpayer dollars.[1]

If the decline in the error rate were associated with a decrease in the number of ineligible families finding their way onto the welfare rolls, then management might well claim credit for saving taxpayer dollars. Unfortunately, caseload data are no less ambiguous than the error rate on this point. The number of families receiving AFDC changed little before, during or after the reform period. (See Table 5.1.) Between 1977 and 1981, approximately 120,000 families received assistance each year. Whether the number of cases would have increased were it not for management's reforms is difficult to assess given the many factors that influence caseload dynamics (such as the economy, demographics, benefit levels, and policy). Notably, even during the height of the error rate crisis, MDPW reformers did not claim credit for this long-term caseload stability.[2]

Even when caseload projections, which incorporate multiple factors, are used, inferences concerning the effects of reform may be inappropriate and misleading. For example, late in 1981, the MDPW reported a short-term caseload reduction for the second quarter of that year (Massachusetts Department of Public Welfare, July 30, 1981). The immediate cause of the decline was a 15.9 percent rise in case closings, which grew more rapidly than new case openings. MDPW analysts noted that nearly half of the closings were attributed to recipient failure to comply with procedural requirements, particularly verification requirements. Families losing benefits for "failure to comply" had increased by 47.3 percent over that category of closings for the previous quarter. MDPW analysts claimed that these data demonstrated that, because of improved local office performance, ineligible persons were being removed from the welfare rolls.

If one assumed that 100 percent of those denied benefits for failure to comply would have been ineligible for AFDC if they had successfully completed all procedural steps, then the "reformed" bureaucracy could, indeed, be credited with doing a better job. However, if this assumption did not hold, then these caseload figures could suggest something quite different—that recipients had lost their benefits on strictly procedural grounds.[3] Unfortunately, neither the department's caseload nor quality control data indicate whether the temporary caseload decline was cause for congratulation or concern. More significant, from a political perspective, the possibility of reform's negative effects was virtually a non-issue for officials and, paradoxically, for the poor.

This points to a more fundamental concern. Assume for the moment that the error rate, however imperfect, can reasonably be interpreted to indicate that excess payments declined, although by less than the error rate indicates. Does this mean, as Commissioner Pratt claimed, that the department's performance improved generally? Or, while errors of liberality declined, did errors of stringency increase? If, as hypothesized earlier, there were a production tradeoff between the two types of error, neither this tradeoff nor its magnitude would be made visible by the error rate, because it measured only excess payments.[4] Consequently, errors of stringency, which may result from extreme caution, increased procedural barriers, or disregard of welfare's "helping" provisions, remain unknown. Yet, given the one-sided thrust of the MDPW's reform program, these unmeasured attributes of performance have critical bearing on the question of administrative "accuracy" and "quality."

By investigating the process through which reforms were translated by the bureaucracy into local office practice, it is possible to gain insights into these unmeasured effects. This chapter turns the analysis of reform's implementation "on its head," re-examining management's initiatives from the bottom up.

## The Bureaucratic Environment

At the heart of management's reform strategy was an effort to circumscribe the discretion exercised by street-level bureaucrats in distributing assistance. The welfare bureaucracy's discretion was not unbounded, even before reform, but was influenced by multiple factors in the work environment as mediated by professional norms and attitudes, personal preferences, and other factors generally beyond management control. As reforms implemented to reduce quality control errors altered the work environment (directly and indirectly), they affected the discretionary behavior of welfare bureaucrats.

Management has the most direct control over the work environment in terms of departmental policies—regulations and rules of practice—and organizational design. As discussed, reformers, with quality control analyses in hand, redrafted policies to increase the stringency of the department's procedural tests of eligibility. In addition, practices were redesigned to minimize the incidence of the "most costly" errors (in terms of quality control sanctions). Rules and regulations were specified, monitored, and enforced by a variety of instruments, including the worker handbook, training programs, and quality assurance.[5] Together, these reform initiatives, at least formally, tightened procedures for screening out overpayments and payments to ineligible persons and explicitly limited worker discretion to deviate from procedural requirements in making benefits decisions.

In moving toward greater uniformity in processing benefits claims, management, in effect, revoked much of the "authorized" discretion that had once been implicit in the job of the welfare worker as social worker. While a broad delegation of decisionmaking authority to a professional "helping" bureaucracy had seemed appropriate, it seemed far less so as the welfare system was reorganized.[6] Counseling functions were transferred to a separate agency that dispensed social services, and the MDPW's function was formally limited to distributing financial assistance. Moreover, the state's high error rate clearly signaled that workers could not be trusted to exercise discretion.

Management not only redesigned policy and practice but also provided standard forms to simplify the worker's task of complying with procedural requirements. For example, workers were required to demand verification of all aspects of eligibility on which payment depended. The central office distributed to workers a checklist of some 35 pieces of evidence that might be necessary to prove eligibility. Redetermination interviews were conducted with reference to a six-page form, which specified questions to be asked of each client and designated a space to note the verification provided in support of their answers. The department also developed form letters, which automatically communicated these requirements. Notices of redetermination sent to clients listed seven documents, which the worker could check off or delete, to be brought to the interview. These forms did not themselves impose requirements, but they reminded workers to follow procedures and made it possible to do so almost automatically. These formal alterations in policy and practice were accompanied by changes in staffing the welfare bureaucracy described earlier. Jobs were formally redefined as clerical, and professional social workers were gradually removed by attrition.

### Error—The Overriding Concern

In many respects, these reforms seemed to disregard tensions implicit in welfare policy—between uniformity and responsiveness to individuals; between assessing claims skeptically and extending assistance to those in need. Management's overriding interest in reducing the error rate was reflected in its one-sided resolution of these conflicting dimensions of welfare administration in favor of greater uniformity and skepticism.

Reformers not only disregarded many aspects of policy delivery that were unrelated to the error rate but also at times purposefully violated department regulations when they appeared to interfere with the war on error. In the case of the enumeration campaign, described earlier, the MDPW permitted workers to accept only a social security card or an ENUM-2 form as evidence that a request for a number was pending. No other evidence, such as a Massachusetts driver's license (which uses a social security number to identify drivers) or even the department's own form (which the ENUM-2 replaced), could be used as verification. However, the "no alternatives" rule issued in a department memorandum was more restrictive than regulations that officially governed department procedures (Massachusetts Department of Public Welfare, Feb. 15, 1980).

Similarly, during Operation Perform, workers were required to make recipients re-register for WIN if their registration forms were more than one year old, and workers were not permitted to accept evidence other than official birth certificates or baptismal certificates to verify grantee ages and relationships. Nevertheless, MDPW regulations continued to require that recipients register only once for WIN and listed 19 types of acceptable verification of age and relationship.[7] Even after these special projects had ended, many workers continued to operate under the impression that the stricter requirements were departmental policy.

In another instance, during the development of the quality assurance review document, one official took the unusual step of questioning a disparity between departmental regulations and management's procedural requirements, as expressed through the quality assurance document review (Massachusetts Department of Public Welfare, Sept. 1979). Quality assurance required evidence that recipients had registered a second time for the WIN program if their cases had been transferred between MDPW offices (usually because of a change in residence). Officials developing the quality assurance system believed that this requirement would reduce quality control errors that occurred because of the department's inability to keep track of WIN records for transferred cases.

However, in an internal memorandum, one official pointed out that MDPW regulations required recipients to register for WIN only once. He questioned whether it was "sound evaluation practice to evaluate perform- ance not spelled out in policy" or whether policy should be revised to be consistent with quality assurance. He did not question whether a policy change that effectively shifted the burden of maintaining registration records from the MDPW to welfare clients was desirable or appropriate.

Subsequently, neither the regulation nor the review document was changed. However, as in the case of the other management initiatives de- scribed previously, policy was rewritten in effect, in this instance by con- tinuing to count in error failure to reverify WIN registration for recipients whose cases were transferred between MDPW offices. In other instances, such as the establishment of the "45–day rule" to define the "currentness" of documents verifying eligibility, official policy was changed after the fact to conform to quality assurance's interpretation of policy in the field. In the ad hoc development of such policies, error was the overriding, if not the only, concern.

## Quality Assurance at the Local Office Level

Despite formal changes in rules, elaboration of quality assurance re- quirements, and the provision of handbooks and worker training, manage- ment could not control the benefits delivery process at the street level for two fundamental and related reasons. The first reason is that discretion is inherent in welfare administration. Policy complexity and ambiguity in family circumstances preclude complete categorization of the choices necessary to make an accurate eligibility determination. Moreover, as noted earlier, wel- fare policy in some respects requires individual treatment of claims and responsiveness to client problems as they are raised. Thus, for policy reasons, worker discretion cannot be eliminated.

Second, in practice administrators depend on workers to exercise dis- cretion in order to "manage" the benefits delivery process. Although workers were formally obliged to observe rules and regulations imposed from above, they were tacitly authorized to use their judgment where rules could not limit the eligibility determination process to a set of simple yes or no choices. For example, it required judgment to decide whether an "absent father" was indeed absent or to interpret the availability of assets in a joint bank account.

Although management necessarily depended on workers to make judgments under such circumstances, it did not trust them to be sufficiently cautious. Management could not be certain that workers would observe (or even understand) specified rules and requirements. Because welfare work consisted not only of paper shuffling, but also of personal interactions between street-level bureaucrats and clients, workers' day-to-day activities were necessarily removed from direct management control. Under these circumstances, workers had many opportunities to exercise "unauthorized" discretion—that is, to act in their own behalf when management and worker interests diverged. Moreover, as is the case for street-level bureaucrats generally, welfare workers had an interest in maintaining discretion as broadly as possible.[8] In this context, reforms that sought to circumscribe discretion by specifying and disseminating policy could not, alone, be expected to have great effect.

However, through quality assurance, management was able to reach down to the local office level much as federal authorities were able to reach out to states through quality control. Quality assurance directly and indirectly altered the bureaucratic environment within which workers exercised discretion in delivering welfare benefits. Quality assurance reviewers assumed much of the tacitly authorized discretion previously exercised by workers in interpreting and applying policy. In addition, quality assurance altered the structure of incentives at the local office level by holding lower-level bureaucrats accountable for observing selected procedural rules.

***Reviewers as Arbiters.*** Reviewers became the arbiters of applied policy by translating policy into practice and enforcing compliance with their interpretations in the course of the review process. As they monitored worker performance, reviewers evaluated individual judgments made in applying welfare policy, focusing on those aspects of policy that were associated with the "most costly" quality control errors. When judgments differed, the process brought these differences—noted as errors—to the attention of local office managers and, subsequently, down the line to unit supervisors and workers.

But, more important than ad hoc correction, through this process, quality assurance's policy interpretations were incorporated into rules of practice by local office administrators and unit supervisors seeking to maximize their performance scores. Not only did quality assurance penetrate deeply to the worker level, but also its influence was broad in scope. Quality assurance reviewers covered up to 80 percent of the redeterminations conducted in the field. As cases were redetermined semi-annually, monitoring extended over most of the MDPW's caseload.[9]

Significantly, quality assurance reviewers approached policy questions from a different perspective than welfare workers. Their mission was to discover worker errors. In the course of their field work, reviewers were embarrassed if their supervisors discovered errors they had missed. Moreover, quality assurance units differed from local office units in the narrowness of their mission—its exclusion of the "helping" dimensions of welfare work— and their distance from welfare recipients. Unlike caseworkers, reviewers answered directly to central management and were physically located in the central office (although they spent considerable time in local offices).[10]

Given the narrowness of the quality assurance reviewers' mission, their role as error "watchdogs," and their insulation from contradictory influences, one would expect them to be more inclined than workers toward procedural stringency. Furthermore, one might expect this bias to be reinforced by the nature of the monitoring task. Reviewers required a consistent set of operational rules in order to conduct their reviews.[11] In the interest of expediting the review process without themselves risking errors, they developed informal rules to simplify their decisionmaking, with rules of local office practice emerging as a result. Rules of practice that emerge through such a process would be apt to look quite different from those established by more highly placed policymakers or social workers.

These differences are illustrated by an encounter observed in one local office between the office administrator and a quality assurance reviewer. The administrator disputed a quality assurance finding that a worker erred in failing to obtain verification that a recipient had registered for the WIN program. The office administrator pointed out that the case record included a dated notation from the worker indicating that he had received verification by telephone from the state employment agency. The quality assurance reviewer acknowledged that both MDPW regulations and the review document stated only that the worker must obtain a "communication" from the agency verifying registration. However, he maintained that the finding of error was appropriate, explaining that "although the manual isn't clear, we've just always taken it to mean that when we say verification, it has to be in writing." He added, "It's not a question of doubting the validity of the verification."

***Supervisors as "Controllers."*** In addition to shifting discretion to interpret policy from welfare workers to reviewers, quality assurance effectively transformed unit supervisors into "error controllers" by holding them accountable for procedural errors made in their units. Supervisors seeking to maximize their units' quality assurance scores were unwilling to sign redeterminations that appeared to contain errors. Moreover, in the face of uncertainty as to how quality assurance reviewers would interpret policy, supervisors tended to be conservative—that is, to err on the side of stringency—in monitoring case processing. From the supervisor's point of view, the case for conservatism was compelling. Supervisors were under intense pressure from office directors, which could manifest itself in embarrassing or threatening demands to explain and remedy high unit error scores or low productivity scores.

Paradoxically, supervisors tended to come from the ranks of social workers, who had tenure in the department from the period preceding the split with the Department of Social Services and who would be precisely those expected to resist the proceduralism and bureaucratization of management's reforms. In fact, some supervisors were uncomfortable with their "controller" role, preferring a more professional, individualized approach to benefits work or even a more lenient one. In interviews, several supervisors clearly expressed conflict between social work and administrative values but also a sense that "supervisors have no choice" in enforcing procedural rules. These contradictory impulses were reflected in comments offered by one supervisor during a discussion of increased verification requirements. Discussing her responsibilities as a supervisor, she asserted that "I watch my workers" and would not approve redeterminations "even if they're just missing a piece of paper, but it doesn't mean anything [substantive with regard to eligibility]." However, when, as a social worker, she and her fellow workers had to demand verifications from clients, she felt that "we were sort of harassing people who needed welfare and were too poor or too honest to cheat."

In effect, quality assurance extended management's reach to the local office level and restructured the work environment by:

- substituting reviewer judgment for worker or supervisor judgment in adapting and interpreting policy;
- narrowing the scope of worker discretion by increasingly specifying acceptable choices, with a bias toward rigid proceduralism; and
- through performance measurement, altering the balance of incentives that influenced worker behavior.

By transferring discretion to a different part of the bureaucracy, one operating with different interests, attitudes, and norms, MDPW reformers indirectly accomplished through quality assurance what others have sought to accomplish more overtly through reorganization. That is, by altering the locus of decisionmaking, they changed the decisions produced by the bureaucracy.

## The Street-Level Response to Reform

As management reforms designated to tighten procedural safeguards against excess payments were translated into practice by successive layers of the bureaucracy, practice increasingly became rulebound and procedurally stringent. Within this constrained environment, workers used their discretion to maximize measured performance and to minimize the cost of responding to the pressures and requirements of administrative reforms.

Redetermination productivity was the yardstick against which worker performance was measured. Lower-level bureaucrats widely recognized what one training supervisor stressed to new workers: "Everything is redeterminations. You could be the worst worker in the world, but if you meet your quota, you can do anything." Few workers doubted that gaining promotion, as well as avoiding probation, depended on production scores. One worker, singled out by colleagues and supervisors as one of the office's "best," explained the importance of redetermination scores in this way: "If you don't meet your quota, people look at the statistics and say 'This is a bad worker'" (interview, 1981).

### Coping, Conservatism, and Consistency

However important, redetermination productivity was only one of many job demands. Special projects (which were also monitored), client requests for assistance, case maintenance, and record-keeping also demanded attention. Behavioral strategies, which workers developed to cope with multiple demands, were adapted to the new mix of incentives, interests, and resources in the reformed work environment. Cumulatively, these coping mechanisms comprised a set of informal, but powerful, rules that structured bureaucratic routine.

The significance of these adaptive responses is highlighted by Lipsky, who points out that "the decisions of street-level bureaucrats, the routines they establish, and the devices they invent to cope with uncertainties and work pressures, effectively become the public policies they carry out" (Lipsky, 1980, p. xii). Consistent with the thrust of MDPW reforms, the administrative routine that emerged from the dialectic between management reforms and bureaucratic adaptations increased procedural barriers to those seeking public assistance without regard to negative effects on those entitled to assistance.

The coping mechanisms, which enabled workers to maximize productivity at minimum cost, can be grouped into two broad categories. One set was composed of shortcuts and informal decision rules that reduced the probability of delays from above, that is, in obtaining supervisory approval of the completed redetermination. The second set reduced the potential for delay from below, that is, from recipients. These were necessary because workers depended on recipients to jump a series of procedural hurdles quickly enough to meet production quota deadlines. They also depended on recipients who could reduce worker productivity by making time-consuming demands.

Under pressure to minimize quality assurance errors, supervisors held workers to a strict standard of procedural compliance. Workers who failed to satisfy these requirements risked having redeterminations returned to them for additional work. Often, if the supervisor demanded additional verification before approving the case, the worker lost several days awaiting the review and then had to depend on the recipients to obtain the necessary documents before the quota deadline expired. Workers preferred to avoid returning with new demands to recipients who had already jumped procedural hoops and had been assured they had fully satisfied the worker's requirements.

To avoid delay and embarrassment, workers tried to anticipate supervisor demands. However, this was often difficult because of uncertainty as to rules and requirements, which frequently changed (or were re-interpreted in quality assurance reviews). In the face of uncertainty, workers could lower the risk of delay by "over-anticipating" supervisor demands. By routinely asking recipients to meet the broadest possible range of procedural requirements, workers could minimize this risk while passing the costs of compliance to the recipient. (Paradoxically, if carried too far, such demands could create delays by making it too difficult or time-consuming for recipients to comply within deadlines.) A shortcut in over-anticipating requirements was to put recipients through a long series of procedural hoops without assessing on an individual basis whether these steps were necessary to determine eligibility. A relatively innocuous practice was to inform clients routinely that all documents listed on a standard redetermination notice were necessary, although a check of the case record might have revealed that some verifications were already in the file.

***The Burden of Proof.*** More serious were demands that substantially increased the recipient's burden of proof, sometimes against an implicit presumption of ineligibility. For example, if recipients fell into certain categories, they might be required to prove that they were ineligible for other benefits and might be sent automatically to apply for benefits, such as veterans' pensions, social security, or unemployment. Thus, if a recipient's husband died, she might be sent to apply for social security death benefits for her children, even if the worker were certain that the children were ineligible, as in the case described earlier. Regardless of the evidence available to workers, they could protect themselves best in these cases by accepting as evidence only a formal rejection letter from the relevant agency. Several workers said it upset them to require recipients needlessly to spend hours wending their way through yet another bureaucracy. But, much like their supervisors, they felt that they had no choice. Whether, in fact, they could exercise discretion to excuse recipients from such requirements, it was certainly less risky to obtain verifications, and the cost of acquiring them could be passed to clients.

Such routines increased the recipient's burden of proof without apparent relevance to the objective of accurate benefits delivery. An observed interaction illustrates this point. In redetermining eligibility, workers confirmed the recipient's residence, customarily requesting two verifications, preferably a rent receipt and a utility bill. In the course of one redetermination, the young woman whose case was under review did not bring a rent receipt to the interview. She explained that she lived in a subsidized apartment and, therefore, did not pay rent. However, the worker refused to accept her telephone and gas bills, each of which contained her name and address, as proof of residence. Instead, he insisted that she provide a letter from her landlord in lieu of a rent receipt. She then explained that her landlord disliked such requests and probably would not respond. Reluctantly, the worker agreed to accept a copy of her lease as a substitute.

Questioned later about this exchange, the worker said that, although he did not doubt her residence, he needed the rent receipt to establish that she received a housing subsidy. However, under further questioning, he acknowledged that, as she had claimed no housing expenses, her rent was not an issue. He then offered an alternative rationale, that he needed a rent receipt or comparable document to avoid a quality assurance error. In fact, quality assurance did not require a rent receipt.

This worker's response was revealing in two respects. First, it suggested the distance between routine procedural demands and questions of substantive eligibility. Second, it reflected a conservative response to confusion and uncertainty about what quality assurance and, more important, unit supervisors would accept as adequate documentation. Notably, confusion of this sort was commonplace despite reforms intended to train workers and keep them up-to-date on welfare policy.

Others have observed similar worker approaches to verification issues. One compilation of verification problems routinely experienced by legal services attorneys across the state noted the following (Sard, 1982):

- refusal to accept a short form certifying birth rather than a longer-form birth certificate;
- failure or refusal to retrieve from the case file documents that clients had provided previously and that were not subject to change (such as social security numbers and birth certificates);
- insistence in the summer months, when schools were closed, on a letter verifying school attendance; and
- general refusal to accept alternative forms of evidence or inform clients of the variety of verifications that were permitted by department regulations.

Although workers could reduce delays from above by observing procedural routines that over-anticipated higher-level demands, such a strategy posed a dilemma to the extent that it increased the likelihood of delays from below. To cope with what some welfare bureaucrats called "the client variable," workers devised strategies to expedite case processing at the client level. In interviews with local office units, several workers proudly described "systems" they had individually devised to speed clients through the redetermination process.

Several coping mechanisms appeared to be commonly employed. For example, workers routinely gave recipients only 3 or 4 days to provide verifications when regulations permitted 10 to 20 days and also permitted extensions, if needed. One worker explained: "We give them 'ample time' to produce verifications. 'Ample time' is your own discretion." Workers also could minimize the cost of enforcing their demands for verification at redetermination by processing termination notices after the 4 days had elapsed. The presumption implicit in this "system" was that recipients would act only under peril of losing their benefits.

Although recipients undoubtedly were responsive to such threats (and some were even aware that they had 30 days to "stop the clock" before the closing automatically took effect), others lost benefits, at least temporarily and at times through no fault of their own. The effects of this type of routine were most serious when verifications were difficult to obtain, especially when they depended on the responses of agencies and people over which the recipients had no control (for example, hospitals, doctors, city halls, or bureaucracies in other countries). Clients' cases would automatically close for "refusal to comply with verification requirements," unless the clients knew that they could request extensions and were able to reach their workers to make a request (which was not always easy to do).[12]

***Caught in the Rush.*** Workers, for the most part, did not intend to harm clients by rushing them through the redetermination process and automatically processing termination papers. Some workers even offered the dubious argument that they were helping their clients by pressuring them to act quickly. Furthermore, when asked, workers seemed to have little notion of the extent to which these practices might have denied benefits to families, who were entitled to and in need of assistance.[13] It may be that the automatic character of the termination process—the fact that workers could dissociate the act of filing a termination notice from the conclusion of that process—partially insulated workers from the consequences of their routine actions. Also, workers could rationalize these practices if they believed, as many did, that recipients would somehow overcome procedural obstacles if they "really needed" or "deserved" assistance. As one worker asserted, "If they don't comply within the deadline, I close them. Either they're trying to hide something, or they just don't care" (interview, 1981).

Many cases continued to be expedited by minimizing individual attention to clients and their procedural difficulties. The capacity of workers to extend help to their clients was effectively limited by their overriding interest in maximizing productivity. In order to cope with productivity demands, workers avoided time-consuming tasks and interactions that could delay or disrupt production. This was true even among workers who expressed concern that clients were unfairly losing benefits because of procedural burdens.

In the absence of countervailing pressures, caseworkers had few incentives to take time to help clients or perform case maintenance functions that would increase assistance to recipients. As one worker who expressed concern about his clients' procedural difficulties explained, "If you're a nice guy and give them an extension, you get yelled at because of the [office] statistics. . . . It gets to the point where you can't be as sympathetic as you ought to be. You don't have the time to do everything." In one Boston office in which the pressure to improve office statistics became particularly intense, one former worker described the situation in this way: "You'd walk down the halls and hear yelling and screaming, and most of it would be the workers. . . . You'd forget. You just thought of the clients as numbers—'Hey, that's my redetermination!'"

Among those who most successfully adapted to the reformed environment were some of the newest workers. After eight months on the job, one young man in his early twenties proudly informed a visitor that his was "the best unit in the office, because we have the fastest turnaround in case actions." He explained that the job consisted mostly of paper processing. "I like to just do the paperwork and let the more compassionate people do the other work. Anyway, the job is structured so it's like a machine. You just have to process the financial work and papers. If I spent three hours talking to someone about their problems, I'd have to explain why I didn't meet my quota."

**The Case of Susan Greene.** Together, incentives to maximize production, disincentives to "bend the rules," and sheer confusion could lead clients and workers into a procedural maze from which escape at times appeared impossible. The case of "Susan Greene" provides an illustrative example.[14] When Susan Greene remarried, she and her two young children from a previous marriage continued to receive AFDC benefits because her new husband, Alan, was unemployed and could not contribute to family support. Mrs. Greene gave birth to a third child in March 1980 and contacted her welfare worker to request that the baby be added to the grant. The increase amounted to about $85 per month, plus Medicaid benefits.

She was informed that first she would have to obtain a birth certificate and social security number for the child. However, she had trouble getting a certificate because the baby was born at home. The worker refused to accept a letter from Mrs. Greene's doctor or an affidavit from a witness to the birth in lieu of a birth certificate or a hospital record, but the worker did not suggest any alternatives either. Mrs. Greene then discovered that she also needed a birth certificate to obtain a social security card for the baby.

Mrs. Greene again spoke to her welfare worker when her case was redetermined late in May, almost three months later. The worker confirmed that Mrs. Greene was still entitled to assistance for herself and her family, but again the worker said that she could not increase the family's grant unless she received a birth certificate for the baby. However, she promised to restore benefits retroactive to the date of birth when the birth certificate was provided.

In February 1981, Mrs. Greene obtained a birth certificate and brought it to her next redetermination in March, nearly one year after the child's birth. She also told the new worker handling her case that she wanted to include her husband in the grant since he was still unable to find work. The worker said that she would have to close the case in order to place the grant in Mr. Greene's name under the terms of the AFDC unemployed parent program (AFDC-UP). She sent Mrs. Greene to an intake worker, who accepted the family's application after Mr. Greene verified his employment history, applied for unemployment compensation, registered for the WIN program, and completed other routine procedural requirements. The intake worker also included the baby in the grant but said she could not provide retroactive benefits to the date of the baby's birth.

With the help of a legal services attorney, the Greenes later appealed the decision to a fair hearing. At the hearing, they requested retroactive benefits beginning with the date of the baby's birth. In her decision, the examiner agreed that the department had violated its own regulations in failing to help the Greenes obtain a birth certificate. However, she ruled against the request for benefits on the grounds that the file did not indicate that Mr. Greene had been categorically eligible for benefits during that period. On appeal to the court, a new fair hearing was ordered. At the second hearing, Mr. Greene testified that he had been unemployed, making the baby eligible for benefits under the AFDC-UP program. The MDPW then dropped its objections and agreed to pay retroactive benefits—17 months, four attorneys, one court appeal, and two hearings after the Greenes first requested assistance for their new baby.

## Institutional Skepticism and Unbounded Suspicion

In a sense, coping mechanisms, which routinely increased obstacles to those seeking assistance, represented the "rational" side of the bureaucratic response to reform. However, there was also an attitudinal dimension. Campaigns against error and fraud and the thrust of the institutional changes described here cued workers that recipients were not to be trusted. Although many welfare workers had long believed this, the management activities initiated to reduce error reinforced these negative attitudes and provided legitimate channels for their expression. This type of attitude was illustrated in an interview with an intake worker who complained that AFDC was too lenient in providing benefits to pregnant women. He contended that reverification of pregnancy every three months was inadequate to prevent fraud, because women would use pregnancy to obtain benefits, then have abortions and collect an additional three months of benefits.[15]

The monthly reverification that he preferred was beyond the range of even "unauthorized" discretion. But in many other areas, workers virtually had free reign to abuse the verification process and express their mistrust and, at times, hostility toward those seeking help. For example, one intake worker, who prided herself on being "very good at finding out which people are telling . . . the truth," described a case that had triggered her suspicion.

The applicant claimed to need assistance for himself and his two children because he had lost his job. At the worker's request, he brought to the office a letter from his employer stating that he no longer worked for the firm and that his last day on the job was several weeks earlier. The caseworker explained that her suspicion was aroused when the letter did not also specify whether the applicant had been fired or laid off. The worker wondered if, perhaps, the applicant had been given a leave of absence and would be returning to work, although there was nothing in the letter to indicate this. She asked the applicant to return with a letter that clarified the circumstances under which his employment had ended. She warned that, unless her doubts were dispelled, she would refuse benefits for "failure to verify potential resources" (a category that did not exist in MDPW regulations).

Another view of this attitudinal dimension of the reformed bureaucracy was provided by an intake supervisor, who was unusually critical of the harsh standards of judgment on which workers (even those in her unit) based their decisions. She regarded many decisions as a product of the worker's subjective assessment of a client's "credibility" and "reasonableness," an assessment she believed was influenced by the work environment. "They think their job is to root out the cheats and frauds," she asserted. "If they don't think that when they get here, they do soon after. That's where the reinforcement is."[16]

Given workers' relative latitude to harass clients with procedural requirements, it is significant that even in extreme cases worker abuse of the verification process could be incredibly difficult to challenge or rectify. One such case totally confounded the legal services advocate who assumed that task.[17] The applicant, "Robert Carver," was a man in his fifties, suffering from severe medical problems, among them a degenerative muscular disease that had prevented him from continuing his work as a laborer. He had sought legal advice on several matters and, in the course of discussion, disclosed the difficulties he was having applying for AFDC for himself, his wife, and their 14–year-old child. He said that he felt he was under suspicion each time the verifications he brought to the worker failed to satisfy her and that he nearly despaired of providing satisfactory documentation of his eligibility.

The advocate, "John Monroe," encouraged him to continue the process and offered to sit down with Mr. Carver and the welfare worker to determine what verifications were necessary to resolve the case. The case was a complicated one. Mr. Carver was claiming AFDC benefits as an unemployed parent, having lost his job as a laborer because of his degenerative muscle disease. His wife was also ill and unable to work. In addition to AFDC, Mr. Carver had requested emergency assistance to avoid eviction from the house in which he and his family had lived for more than 10 years. He had been unable to pay rent since losing his only source of income several months earlier.

The worker told Mr. Carver and his attorney, Mr. Monroe, that the following verifications were needed:

- a current statement of Mrs. Carver's bank account;
- a medical form signed by Mr. Carver's doctor (the doctor had previously submitted a six-page, single-spaced statement detailing his patient's condition and the prognosis that it was degenerative);
- a statement from Mrs. Carver's doctor explaining her illness; and
- a notice of eviction and a letter from the landlord's attorney stating that he would execute the eviction within a month if the rent were not paid and confirming that Mr. Carver had paid $700 in back rent the previous month.

A few days later, Mr. Carver received a note from his welfare worker formally extending the application deadline to permit further verification and confirming the request for Mrs. Carver's bank statement, medical verifications for Mr. and Mrs. Carver, an eviction notice, and a rent receipt. In the note, the worker also asked for verification of Mrs. Carver's work history for the previous year, which, the worker wrote, "I forgot to request."

Several days later, Mr. Monroe brought the first four items to the office. (The landlord's letter satisfied the demand for a rent receipt.) He explained that in a previous discussion, the assistant director of the welfare office had agreed that Mrs. Carver's work history was not relevant to the application and suggested the worker confirm that conversation with him. However, the worker was also dissatisfied with the response to her other requests. She said the medical verifications were "incomplete," that she needed additional details on a car accident in which Mrs. Carver had been hurt the previous year and that she wanted a bank statement for another account that had already been verified with a letter of balance from the bank.

The advocate returned to the doctor, who wrote another letter explaining his diagnosis of Mr. Carver's illness and attached x-rays.[18] He also obtained the bank statement, additional information for completing MDPW medical forms, and an affidavit from the attorney who handled the insurance claim from Mrs. Carver's accident. The advocate had Mr. Carver sign a letter agreeing to permit the welfare office to contact his doctors directly. Before bringing these materials to the welfare office, the advocate called and was told to obtain a letter from Mr. Carver permitting the worker to discuss his case with the advocate. Mr. Monroe had such a letter prepared and signed by Mr. Carver, although the advocate had previously submitted notice of representation to the welfare office.

That afternoon, Mr. Monroe again met with the worker, who contended that the medical information was still incomplete and asked for two additional documents: one, a statement from the landlord explaining why he continued to rent to the Carver family after moving to evict them once before when they had fallen behind in their rent and, two, lapsed insurance policies that the Carvers acknowledged having had several years before. The worker said that she would not accept Mr. Carver's application for emergency assistance and that she intended to deny the application for AFDC (even if the two additional documents were provided) because she did not regard the medical evaluation as sufficient proof that Mr. Carver could not work. The worker also refused the advocate's request for a speedy denial so that the matter could be taken to a fair hearing, perhaps in time to avoid eviction. The office director, who was called into the dispute, supported the worker's actions.

As the case dragged on, Mr. Carver became less willing to return to the welfare office, explaining that he felt humiliated by the constant suspicion and reluctant to continue asking children and friends for transportation to the office. He finally asked that the case be dropped. Subsequently, he and his family were evicted. His wife and younger child went to live with one of their older children, and Mr. Carver entered the hospital.

Mr. Carver's request for assistance fell into that subjective category of cases that arouse the suspicion, rather than the sympathies, of welfare workers. Unlike Mrs. Greene's caseworkers, who felt themselves caught in procedural rules, the welfare bureaucrats who handled Mr. Carver's case used those rules to construct an elaborate barricade, which kept him from obtaining assistance. Certainly, worker suspicion and abuses of discretion were not new. But it is significant that, even in the reformed bureaucracy, workers maintained virtually unlimited discretion to doubt claims of eligibility and to shield their actions under cover of stringent departmental verification requirements.

## Adding Up Reform's Effects

In a sense, management's error-reducing reforms served their manifest purpose. Workers paid attention to both productivity and procedural requirements, which penetrated the local office level through quality assurance. In fact, incentives in the reformed bureaucracy were so heavily weighted toward satisfying these requirements that concern with other aspects of welfare production was virtually displaced. Workers behaved as if there were a tradeoff (such as that hypothesized by Mills) between helping clients to obtain benefits and screening the claims of those who were not entitled to receive assistance.

However, this tradeoff was largely unrecognized, in part because it occurred as a by-product of day-to-day decisions made on other grounds. Workers' decisions were not generally made in terms of their outcomes— that is, whether clients received too much or too little. Rather, procedural compliance—"going through all the steps"—was, itself, an objective. Routine decisions reflected workers' conservatism in the face of uncertainty as to the attributes of procedural "accuracy." These decisions also reflected a rational assessment of the relatively low cost (to the worker) of making errors of stringency. By making decisions that erred on the side of stringency, workers could satisfy performance demands and appear to be delivering welfare more accurately, according to quantitative indicators.

## The Distributive Effects of Stringency

However, beyond reform's measured effect of reducing the error rate, increased procedural stringency produced unmeasured distributive effects. The procedural "screen" through which claims were filtered effectively became more dense, making it harder for claimants to obtain benefits. Workers routinely applied stringent verification rules and sent clients from office to office to obtain documents (for example, birth certificates, social security cards, applications for veterans' benefits) without first considering whether those documents were needed to determine eligibility. Observing at least the superficial terms of the department's "prudent standard," workers accepted only specified verifications without making judgments about the validity of client assertions.

These types of practices effectively increased the "cost" to clients of obtaining benefits and even shifted some administrative costs from the department to its clients. For example, the cost of poorly maintained case records was effectively shifted to clients when workers asked them to obtain documents without first checking through masses of unsorted case records or when the department required that they re-register for WIN if their cases were transferred between offices. Clients were also expected to assume the dollar costs of verifying eligibility, among them document fees, transportation, and, for working recipients, time off from their jobs.

Although individuals are generally expected to absorb some costs in obtaining citizenship benefits, the level and allocation of those costs are essentially political decisions. They affect the consumption of benefits by making them anything from a free good to virtually unaffordable (Prottas, 1981). However, "entitlements" are imbued with the presumption that citizens who meet certain categorical and financial standards have a "right" to receive benefits. Thus, adding substantial procedural costs to the acquisition of a social entitlement is different from, say, imposing user fees for public transportation. It is, in effect, rationing by the back door.[19]

Furthermore, costs assessed through procedural requirements diminish equity in welfare distribution, because they are allocated differentially and without regard to ability to pay. The highest costs were "charged" to clients who, by chance, fell into certain categories, for example: clients with earnings, who had to obtain wage stubs and detailed evidence of work expenses; clients, such as Mrs. Greene, who could not easily obtain a standard birth certificate; or applicants like Mr. Carver, who aroused worker suspicion and whose case raised complicated issues.

Clients also varied in their capacity to absorb procedural (and sometimes psychic) costs associated with obtaining welfare in the reformed bureaucracy (Goodban, 1981). While some recipients undoubtedly became relatively adept at negotiating the welfare system, others found it unfathomable. (At times, workers were as baffled by complex and frequently changing rules, compounding problems for their clients.) One federal commission that studied this problem concluded that "those most in need of assistance are often the least able to complete the forms and procedures necessary to receive assistance" (Commission on Federal Paperwork, 1977, p. 25).

Further evidence on this point comes from an analysis of the Colorado monthly reporting system experiment. This system required recipients to mail forms to the welfare office each month with up-to-date information on a variety of aspects of eligibility, including verification of wages, work expenses, and so forth. By keeping records current, monthly reporting was ostensibly designed to reduce payment errors. However, David Price's analysis (1981) of the Colorado experiment indicated that monthly reporting procedures screened out some clients without regard to substantive eligibility. He estimated that 20 to 50 percent of recipients denied benefits for failing to meet procedural requirements were otherwise entitled to assistance. Procedural barriers had the strongest screening effect on poorly educated, non-English speaking recipients. Ironically, in the absence of comparable data for non-monthly reporting welfare offices, Price could not say whether procedural barriers to welfare were any less severe, generally.

Clearly, in Massachusetts, reformed bureaucratic practices made it harder for many individuals to obtain welfare, because procedural costs increased and worker assistance declined. Although this outcome may be undesirable, it might be acceptable if it provided a more accurate distribution of benefits. However, this does not appear to be the case. The bureaucratic routine that developed in response to reform appears to have systematically created barriers, which were purported to screen only ineligible claimants but, in practice, screened eligible ones as well. As one former welfare official remarked caustically, "You can get the error rate down to zero, but you'll only have 10 clients left" (interview, 1982).

## Estimating the Magnitude of Unmeasured Effects

Because quality control measures only "excess" payments, it is not possible to determine the extent to which benefits were improperly denied and delayed or individuals were discouraged from seeking assistance. However, fragmentary evidence assembled over the course of this inquiry provides additional insights into the unmeasured effects of error-reducing reforms. Suggestive, but ambiguous, data can be gleaned from the MDPW's own records, which indicate an increase in applications denied over the course of the reform period. This increase in denials was led by an increase in rejections based on the applicant's "failure to comply" with procedural requirements. (See Table 6.1.) In late 1977, "failure to comply" was the reason cited for 38 percent of all denials. But it accounted for 57 percent of

**Table 6.1**

Procedural Denials by Quarter for Massachusetts and the Boston Region:
November 1977–September 1980

| Year–Quarter | Massachusetts | | | Boston Region | | |
|---|---|---|---|---|---|---|
| | % of Applications Denied* | % of Applications Denied/ Proced.† | % of Denials/ Proced.‡ | % of Applications Denied* | % of Applications Denied/ Proced.† | % of Denials/ Proced.‡ |
| 1977–4th | 18 | 7 | 38 | 21 | 13 | 58 |
| 1978–1st | 18 | 7 | 34 | 20 | 16 | 75 |
| 1978–2nd | 19 | 8 | 40 | 26 | 16 | 62 |
| 1978–3rd | 19 | 8 | 41 | 26 | 15 | 58 |
| 1978–4th | 21 | 10 | 46 | 29 | 19 | 64 |
| 1979–1st | 20 | 10 | 46 | 28 | 19 | 65 |
| 1979–2nd | 20 | 9 | 42 | 29 | 19 | 66 |
| 1979–3rd | 22 | 11 | 48 | 31 | 20 | 63 |
| 1979–4th | 22 | 11 | 50 | 31 | 23 | 75 |
| 1980–1st | 23 | 13 | 54 | 31 | 23 | 73 |
| 1980–2nd | 18 | 12 | 55 | 29 | 22 | 75 |
| 1980–3rd | 22 | 13 | 57 | 28 | 21 | 71 |

Source: Massachusetts Department of Public Welfare, 3800 Reports.
* Percent denied of all applications processed.
† Percent denied for procedural reasons (failiure to comply or failure to verify) of all applications processed.
‡ Percent of all denials attributed to procedural reasons (compliance or verification).

the denials three years later. The figures for Boston welfare offices are more striking. These offices, which account for one-quarter of the state's AFDC caseload, were the first and primary targets of management's anti-error drive. In Boston, denials rose by almost 10 percent between 1977 and 1980, and the proportion of procedural denials increased (with interim variations) from about 58 to 71 percent.

Yet, it remains unclear whether these figures should be interpreted to indicate an increase in errors of stringency—that is, denials occurring irrespective of categorical or financial eligibility. Fortunately, Hecker and Nelson's analysis (1981) of Boston fair hearing decisions for 1978 to 1980 bears directly on this question. They found that worker decisions to deny benefits for procedural non-compliance were overturned at an increasing rate during this period. Fair hearing examiners sustained client challenges in 59 percent of cases denied in 1978, 68 percent in 1979, and 64 percent in 1980. When the central issue in denials involved verification, appeals were sustained in 56 percent of fair hearings in 1978, 67 percent in 1979, and 70 percent in 1980. Hecker and Nelson attribute the increase in apparently erroneous denials to increased procedural stringency at the local office level. Their findings are consistent with other evidence in this study.

Fair hearing data, however, provide only a crude indicator of the extent to which errors of stringency occurred, primarily because the fair hearing "sample" is self-selected.[20]

Hecker and Nelson's findings are also intriguing with regard to the proposition that fair hearings provide a "safety valve" that ameliorates the worst effects of increased agency stringency. As Nonet pointed out in another context, quasi-judicial administrative proceedings may perform the latent function of making "ad hoc accommodations that escape scrutiny and prevent the criticism and elaboration of policy" (Nonet, 1969, p. 226). This view certainly applies to welfare regulations that make fair hearing decisions case-specific (that is, they have no value as precedents) and to apparent management disinterest in aggregating fair hearing decisions as a tool for evaluating department policies and practices.

Another indicator of improperly denied or delayed benefits is "churning"—the termination and rapid reinstatement of families from the welfare rolls. Churning generally indicates that families were temporarily dropped from the rolls until they could complete procedural requirements. Data collected from the Roxbury Crossing welfare office in Boston indicate varying amounts of churning during 1980, a period during which that office was a frequent target of experimental initiatives to reduce error as well as a participant in state-wide reforms. Although the number of terminations in that one office was fairly low, the percentage of cases reopened within one month of closing ranged from 6 to 32 percent, with a median churning rate of 19 percent.[21]

Caseload, fair hearing, or other available data (such as rates of procedural denials) were not systematically collected and analyzed by the MDPW to determine whether the department was delivering benefits "accurately." Officials not only relied on the error rate as the measure of administrative performance but also claimed to be unaware that unmeasured errors of stringency could be occurring. One of the highest state officials involved in the reform effort appeared genuinely surprised when asked during an interview whether clients may have been harmed. "It is not an issue which ever came up," he said after a brief pause.

In 1979 the "error rate crisis" provoked a substantial effort toward administrative reform in Massachusetts. The need for reform was unarguable, given a system characterized by bureaucratic arbitrariness, delay, and confusion. However, officials became immersed in an assault on quality control errors without, it seems, ever asking, "What kind of reform is this?" In the abstract, it was quite reasonable to argue, as did Commissioner Pratt, that in lowering the error rate, reformers would restore welfare's legitimacy and, thus, protect it from attacks that used mismanagement and fraud as weapons. Furthermore, reform would protect welfare recipients who often suffered abuse at the hands of lower-level welfare workers.

However, if reformers' underlying concerns were welfare's political legitimacy and administrative fairness, should they not have been alarmed at indications that these concerns were being distorted in the course of reform by workers' excessive proceduralism, stringency, and disregard for welfare's helping provisions? Perhaps. But officials' apparent lack of alarm may be more a matter of the invisibility of reform's adverse effects than of cynicism and hypocrisy on the part of most welfare reformers. Quality control data indicated that reform was working and that administrative "accuracy" was improving. Errors of stringency were unmeasured and their extent unknown, although not unknowable.[22]

Yet, who was to raise the issue that reform might be denying welfare to eligible families and that reform's adverse effects were sufficient to warrant management's attention? Welfare officials seemed to depend on recipients to perform this function. In an interview with an official in HEW's Boston office, questions about reform's possible adverse effects evoked this response: "If these things are going on, why aren't recipients marching to my office and sitting in the corridors [in protest]?" Officials from HEW's Washington offices replied similarly when asked about the possibility that one-sided reforms might make the system excessively stringent. As one official assured me, "if there were problems, I would have heard about them."

If officials were depending on the victims of their administrative policies to draw attention to the adverse effects of reform, their expectations were unfounded. Aggregate adverse effects were hidden, even from welfare clients who experienced procedural difficulties as individuals. In the absence of aggregate data or organized means of sharing information about individual experiences (for example, through active welfare rights organizations), the systematic effects of administrative reforms were obscured.

Welfare recipients can speak for themselves. But, like public administrators, without data they were unlikely to observe independently or certainly to document the adverse systematic effects of gradually tightening bureaucratic procedures.

### The Error of Their Ways

This case study has followed quality control from its development as part of a federal effort to contain welfare spending to its street-level influence on the provision of welfare. The links between the two, although indirect and often indistinct, were made visible by evaluating the political objectives embedded in quality control's design and examining how quality control influenced administrative reform in Massachusetts. State reforms that standardized, simplified, and tightened administrative procedures were consistent with quality control's emphasis on errors of liberality and its disregard for errors of stringency. That emphasis eventually was reflected in the practices of lower-level workers, although few understood what quality control was or were concerned directly with avoiding errors for which the states could be penalized.

This chapter has been concerned with reform's "invisible" effects and the ways in which poor families and welfare administrators experienced them. It is ironic that when asked about possible adverse effects of their reforms, officials, who had marshaled the technical and administrative resources of their agencies to uncover and eliminate quality control errors, professed to rely on recipients for this information. It seems fitting that, in the final analysis, these officials reached out to blame the victims of administrative reform for failing to draw the attention of reformers to the error of their ways.

# 7

# The "Nonpolitics" of Administrative Reform

Administrative reform promised to improve accuracy and uniformity in state welfare delivery. These objectives were unassailable on their face. Whether one's political preference were for a more or a less generous welfare policy, one could agree that states should provide benefits only to those entitled to receive them and, further, that the task of improving payment accuracy was a managerial one, largely outside the realm of political controversy.

In order to be effective in improving welfare delivery nationally, administrative reform had to reach those high caseload, high error states—like Massachusetts—that accounted for the worst management problems and the largest share of misspent federal dollars. In this respect, administrative reform was an apparent success. Quality control data indicate that the "improvement" achieved in Massachusetts—a 67 percent drop in the error rate in two years—was unusual only in its speed. Nationally, error rates declined more than 50 percent between 1973 (when quality control sanctions were first promulgated) and 1981. At minimum, these figures affirm the potency of performance measurement as an instrument of managerial control.

But, as with other performance measures, the distinction between outputs and outcomes is a critical one. Design flaws in the measurement of error (described in Chapter Four) and quality control's biased influence on state-level reform (discussed in Chapter Six) suggest that an unwarranted leap of faith is required to credit reductions in the error rate with similar improvements in administrative performance or with equivalent levels of tax savings. In contrast, the Massachusetts case strongly suggests that initiatives implemented to reduce error rates may have worsened administrative performance with respect to errors of stringency and, possibly, achieved "savings" by reducing participation in AFDC among eligible families.

## The Record Across the States

In the absence of rigorous studies of the reform process and its un-measured effects in other states, it is difficult to generalize from the Massachusetts case. However, a growing body of fragmentary evidence from other states suggests the Massachusetts experience was not unique. There is considerable evidence of "diffusion of innovation" as states shared information on error-reducing techniques. The American Public Welfare Association's (APWA, 1981) survey of state cost-cutting measures indicates that welfare managers across the country selected techniques from among a common menu of devices. The overlap between reforms initiated as cost-cutting measures and those implemented under the rubric of error reduction seems more than coincidental.[1] The APWA survey also confirms the desperate intensity of the Massachusetts reform drive. Massachusetts employed nearly every device listed in the survey.

The National Academy of Public Administration's (NAPA) case studies of error reduction efforts in eight states (including Massachusetts) reveal an intriguing degree of consistency in the thrust of state reforms. Managerial initiatives in Washington, Wisconsin, Michigan, California, Georgia, Texas, and Illinois were consistent with a general movement toward greater uniformity, routinization and stringency in welfare administration (Zeller, 1981).[2] The NAPA studies do not attempt to assess fully the outcomes of reform. However, a few of the case studies hint at reform's adverse consequences.

For example, Richard Weatherly describes officials in Washington state as trapped by a dilemma, unable to "implement changes which might help reduce error *and* improve services to clients. The agency, facing the threat of sanctions, is forced to invoke measures which are of dubious benefit, but which are ones they can implement" (Weatherly, 1980, p. 33). In Michigan, Daniel Steinmetz observed: "It is not official policy to use procedural requirements to obstruct access to the agency. However, obstructed access has been an unintended consequence of the error reduction drive because that is one of the few devices employees can use to cope with workload pressures" (Steinmetz, 1980, p. 35).

Other studies, some by welfare advocates, have tried to document administrative abuses and their client impact. Project Fair Play investigated welfare administration in six midwestern states and found major barriers to access (Vesely et al., 1982). Among them were lengthy application forms that "require reading at levels well beyond the skills of applicants," "discretionary, burdensome and often unnecessary verification requirements," and minimal or erroneous communication of information needed by clients in order to claim welfare.[3] The report concludes that "armed with inadequate and sometimes mistaken information, AFDC families cannot evaluate decisions made regarding their situation and cannot effectively question the system" (Vesely et al., 1982, p. 9). The "horror stories" of administrative abuse recounted in the report could be regarded merely as anecdotal and exceptional. However, many of these accounts are strikingly familiar and consistent with the systematic effects of stringency-oriented practices, like those observed in Massachusetts.[4]

In response to accusations of an administrative campaign against welfare recipients in New York City, the New York State Department of Social Services conducted its own investigation into case closings in 1983. The state agency found that one consequence of the city's campaign to reduce its error rate was an increase in case closings, one-quarter of which were erroneous and an additional one-third of which were questionable (New York State Department of Social Services, April 1984).[5]

The New York data on case closings may be only the tip of the iceberg. Research by McDonald and Piliavin in Wisconsin suggests that barriers to entry may be an even more severe problem. They examined the 30 percent of applicants who did not complete the application process in Wisconsin and found that at least 35 percent of the non-returnees were apparently eligible for assistance. Their withdrawal from the application process, despite an average potential increase of 62 percent in income, appeared to be related to difficulty negotiating administrative procedures, discomfort with client-worker interactions, and perceptions of stigma (McDonald and Piliavin, 1984).

In a saga laced with irony, it seems fitting that several of these studies conclude by urging that quality control be redesigned to balance concern for errors of liberality with concern for errors of stringency. That such an obvious step has not been taken since sanctions were first attached to quality control in 1973 can only be explained politically.

## Administrative Reform in Political Perspective

Quality control, and the administrative reforms it inspired, did not burst forth from some technocratic vacuum. They had their origins in the welfare explosion and the sense of crisis created in its aftermath.

In a sense, AFDC's rapid growth at the end of the sixties had produced, not one, but two related welfare crises. One was a managerial crisis, provoked by the apparent inability of state officials to control demands for welfare and keep their programs relatively free from fraud, waste and abuse. The other was a political crisis, resulting from congressional failure to agree on a comprehensive reform plan that might simplify welfare management and limit welfare costs.

It was within this specific context that administrative reform developed as a mechanism that enabled federal authorities to indirectly assert their interests in tightening state welfare management and containing welfare costs. Moreover, this mechanism avoided contentious political questions of welfare's appropriate size, scope and terms. Conceivably, reform could have embodied a different balance of concerns. But the definition imparted to reform as it developed at the federal level and was implemented at the state level was consistent with a restrictive response to welfare's growth. While the intent of reformers at various levels of government may be arguable, it is significant that officials behaved as if they were trying to limit welfare's distribution.[6]

Of course, there was an element of intentionality in the evolution of administrative reform. The device of quality control sanctions was conceived originally as part of the Nixon Administration's intentional strategy to assert its policy objectives through bureaucratic means. One may doubt, as I do, that the Nixon Administration over time could have orchestrated the transformation of quality control into street-level restrictions on welfare. However, once in place, quality control established a framework within which administrative reform became defined as an attack on certain types of payment errors. Quality control regularly churned out data on state error rates and presented a threat of fiscal sanctions that federal and state welfare managers could ignore at their peril.

In this sense, reform had many of the attributes that Murray Edelman ascribes to political symbols, highlighting some "facts" and obscuring others (Edelman, 1977). Politicians, of course, are not unaware of the strategic value of such symbols. Nor were they unaware of quality control's political utility. After the demise of the Nixon Administration, anti-welfare congressmen revived quality control as an instrument for attacking HEW's social welfare budget. During the Carter presidency, liberals at HEW sought to use evidence of errors and mismanagement to promote progressive welfare reform. But the mismanagement issue was more amenable to restricting welfare than to expanding or protecting it. As a frame of reference for policy politics, it was distinctly different from the issues of poverty, equality, and the family that defined struggles to expand welfare in the sixties.

Administrative reform's symbolic value contributed to its instrumental utility as a mechanism for responding restrictively to welfare's growth. Piven and Cloward (1971) point out that administrative barriers constitute a secondary line of defense against access to welfare during periods of contraction. But, in the seventies, administrative reform constituted a primary means of limiting access. In this context, it seems appropriate to view administrative reform as an adaptive alternative to "normal" political channels of policymaking and to try to specify what kind of alternative it was.

## The Administrative Alternative: Advantages and Limits

Administrative reform provided a means of circumventing legislative obstacles to policy change and avoiding direct conflict over what welfare policy should be. Among its strategic attributes were, first, that its manifest purposes—administrative accuracy, and fiscal accountability—were nonpolitical and consensual. Second, it operated through technical and bureaucratic processes that masked allocative choices and did not require federal or state legislators to confront contentious policy issues. Third, its systematic effects, produced through apparently uncoordinated lower-level bureaucratic behaviors, were unmeasured and generally unrecognized.

From this political perspective, reform's effectiveness depended on its ability to narrow the scope of conflict over restrictions on welfare while working directly through the institutions that implement policy to redefine entitlements. Administrative reform reduced the risk of countermobilization against restrictions on welfare, in part because it did not overtly breach the integrity of *theoretical entitlement* to welfare promised by statute and supported by law, while in practice initiating a process of *effective disentitlement*. Because reform did not manifestly undermine theoretical entitlement, government institutions and officials were insulated from the effects of their actions. In this sense, reform eroded government accountability that it was ostensibly intended to improve.

It is simply inappropriate to treat reform's restrictive effects on the provision of welfare as "unanticipated consequences" of reform's implementation. Beyond issues previously discussed, one would have to contend with the fact that restrictive consequences could have been and were anticipated by HEW's own consultants, who advised correcting quality control's imbalance.[7] It is not appropriate either to regard these consequences as evidence of democratic responsiveness, assuming that restricting welfare was "an idea whose time had come." If this were the case, why couldn't this "idea" be acknowledged politically? One might even imagine that such an idea would create congressional competition to claim credit for restricting welfare. In marked contrast, administrative reform avoided overt policy politics, translated essentially allocative issues (that is, how accessible welfare should be) into administrative ones, and obscured de facto restrictions on the meaning of welfare entitlements.[8]

But as an alternative means of restricting social entitlements, administrative reform is not without its limits. First, the constituency for welfare, the poor, are more vulnerable politically than other beneficiaries of the social welfare state. As discussed, they are disadvantaged in terms of their socioeconomic position, resources, self-image, and political status. Other target groups may be less vulnerable, particularly those groups regarded as the "deserving poor" and, of course, the non-poor. Second, administrative reform depended on its symbolic appeal and nonpolitical appearance. Policymaking channeled through such mechanisms is necessarily indirect, relatively modest, and blunt-edged. One might regard the type of restrictions imposed through administrative welfare reform as "problematic disentitlement" in contrast to categorical disentitlement, which is more precisely targeted and potentially of broader and more immediate effect (Brodkin and Lipsky, 1983). It is more direct, for example, to eliminate eligibility for categories of beneficiaries, such as children over age 18 who are still in school.

The strategic value of administrative mechanisms appears to erode if pushed too far or targeted against groups that are better able than the poor to fight back. For example, the Reagan Administration's directives redefining and narrowing eligibility criteria for disability benefits touched off a political furor in 1983.[9] The visibility of this strategy undermined its nonpolitical appearance. Its dramatic impact on the disabled made all too clear that there was more to the Administration's "clean up" of the disability rolls than met the eye. Moreover, the disabled are among the "deserving poor" who are able to generate considerable political support. Ultimately, the Administration was forced to capitulate substantially under pressure to restore benefits.

## What Fate for Quality Control?

Even quality control may have lost much of its usefulness as a mechanism for asserting federal control over state welfare programs, in part because it was pushed so far that states developed an urgent interest in fighting it. In 1985, for the first time since the Nixon years, federal authorities attempted to apply fiscal penalties against states that had exceeded allowable error rates. Under the terms of the Michel Amendment, the Department of Health and Human Services (HHS) levied some $73 million in fiscal sanctions against 28 states.[10] (See Table 7.1.) California was hardest hit this time, tallying more than $35 million in penalties. After HHS announced the penalties, a New York Times editorial accused the Reagan Administration of "abusing the war on welfare abuse," commenting that "the Administration dismisses opponents of its inflated fines as soft on welfare fraud. In fact, they are properly offended by an attempt to turn a useful tool into a destructive budget ax."[11]

But that was only the initial sally in this new phase of the protracted war on error. For subsequent fiscal years, rules become even tougher. For fiscal year 1984, states were to be held accountable for achieving a 3 percent target error rate. At this writing, 48 states would be subject to fiscal sanctions on the basis of their 1984 error rates, a situation that Congress seemed unlikely to permit. (See Table 7.2.) In December 1985, Congress placed a six month moratorium on quality control sanctions in the food stamp program and, in March 1986, instituted a two-year moratorium on sanctions in AFDC. Congress also ordered independent studies of quality control and directed HHS to use these studies as the basis for rewriting fiscal sanctions regulations for AFDC, food stamps and Medicaid.

On another battlefront, 29 states, the District of Columbia, and several California counties sued in federal district court to prevent HHS from implementing the fiscal penalties it had announced for AFDC. Reminiscent of the states' successful 1975 lawsuit, the 1986 suit again argued that quality control sanctions were arbitrary and capricious.

Quality control probably will continue to be used as an instrument for monitoring state welfare payments. But its importance as a political mechanism for limiting the provision of welfare has diminished for two reasons.

**Table 7.1**

AFDC Quality Control Error Rates, Target Rates,* and Disallowances by U.S.
and State: Fiscal Year 1981

| | PAYMENT ERROR RATE FISCAL YEAR 1981 | TARGET RATE | POTENTIAL DISALLOW- ANCE AMOUNT (000) |
|---|---|---|---|
| U.S. Total | 7.6 | | 73,502 |
| Alabama | 7.7 | 7.6 | 47 |
| Alaska | 18.2 | 22.1 | — |
| Arizona | 8.3 | 6.7 | 209 |
| Arkansas | 6.8 | 7.4 | — |
| California | 6.8 | 4.0 | 35,067 |
| Colorado | 8.2 | 4.2 | 1,898 |
| Connecticut | 7.4 | 7.1 | 313 |
| Delaware | 11.3 | 12.0 | — |
| District of Columbia | 13.6 | 16.3 | — |
| Florida | 7.9 | 5.1 | 3,467 |
| Georgia | 6.5 | 6.5 | — |
| Hawaii | 10.1 | 7.5 | 1,212 |
| Idaho | 9.1 | 4.3 | 691 |
| Illinois | 8.3 | 12.7 | — |
| Indiana | 4.1 | 4.0 | 113 |
| Iowa | 4.3 | 6.5 | — |
| Kansas | 8.1 | 4.1 | 1,903 |
| Kentucky | 5.0 | 8.1 | — |
| Louisiana | 6.7 | 8.7 | — |
| Maine | 7.9 | 7.5 | 160 |
| Maryland | 11.6 | 10.4 | 1,325 |
| Massachusetts | 9.3 | 11.9 | — |
| Michigan | 7.3 | 7.5 | — |
| Minnesota | 4.4 | 4.0 | 571 |
| Mississippi | 6.9 | 9.0 | — |
| Missouri | 7.1 | 8.1 | — |
| Montana | 4.9 | 7.8 | — |
| Nebraska | 5.5 | 4.4 | 280 |
| Nevada | 2.3 | 4.0 | — |
| New Hampshire | 6.6 | 8.7 | — |
| New Jersey | 8.0 | 7.5 | 1,280 |
| New Mexico | 12.4 | 4.5 | 2,554 |
| New York | 8.0 | 7.2 | 6,270 |
| North Carolina | 5.4 | 6.6 | — |
| North Dakota | 3.1 | 4.0 | — |
| Ohio | 8.9 | 7.7 | 3,930 |
| Oklahoma | 6.6 | 4.0 | 1,508 |
| Oregon | 6.8 | 9.8 | — |

**Table 7.1** (*cont.*)

|  | PAYMENT ERROR RATE FISCAL YEAR 1981 | TARGET RATE | POTENTIAL DISALLOW-ANCE AMOUNT (000) |
|---|---|---|---|
| Pennsylvania | 9.0 | 12.2 | — |
| Puerto Rico | 8.9 | 6.6 | 1,714 |
| Rhode Island | 6.3 | 9.8 | — |
| South Carolina | 7.8 | 6.1 | 1,004 |
| South Dakota | 4.6 | 4.5 | 13 |
| Tennessee | 8.9 | 6.0 | 1,754 |
| Texas | 7.5 | 5.9 | 1,112 |
| Utah | 4.9 | 4.0 | 300 |
| Vermont | 5.2 | 4.3 | 225 |
| Virgin Islands | 6.9 | 8.8 | — |
| Virginia | 3.6 | 9.1 | — |
| Washington | 9.3 | 5.8 | 4,162 |
| West Virginia | 7.4 | 8.9 | — |
| Wisconsin | 8.2 | 8.7 | — |
| Wyoming | 13.7 | 4.0 | 413 |

Source U.S. Department of Health and Human Services
* Target error rates for Fiscal Year 1981 were established under the provisions of the Michel Amendment.

First, as discussed, it has been pushed so far that it has become politicized and has engendered concerted and capable state opposition. In order to provide an effective alternative to policy politics, administrative mechanisms must remain modest in scope and impact.

Second, the political conditions which produced quality control have changed. I have argued that administrative reform developed in response to the welfare crises of the seventies. In the eighties, although poverty rates appear to be rising, welfare rolls have stabilized, and even declined slightly, in part because of legislative restrictions enacted during the Reagan Administration's first term.[12] One should expect an alternative to political forms of policymaking to be adaptive to its particular context. In this new context, administrative barriers to welfare again may assume secondary importance.

## Reform: Its Promise and Possibilities

Promises to root out fraud, waste and abuse and improve the efficiency of social programs have obvious appeal. But the meaning of these promises, in reality, depends on the specific steps taken to translate reform into bureaucratic practice. Ultimately, administrative reforms that alter the delivery of social benefits also change their distribution and even the meaning of

**Table 7.2**

AFDC Quality Control Error Rates and Target Rates by State:
Fiscal Years 1982–1984

| | 1982 | | 1983 | | 1984 | |
|---|---|---|---|---|---|---|
| | Error Rates | Target Rates | Error Rates | Target Rates | Error Rates | Target Rates |
| U.S. Total | 6.9 | | 6.5 | 4.0 | 6.0 | |
| Alabama | 5.3 | 5.8 | 3.2 | 4.0 | 4.4 | 3.0 |
| Alaska | 12.1 | 13.1 | 15.5 | 4.0 | 6.8 | 3.0 |
| Arizona | 11.6 | 5.3 | 10.0 | 4.0 | 9.7 | 3.0 |
| Arkansas | 7.0 | 5.7 | 4.9 | 4.0 | 3.8 | 3.0 |
| California | 6.0 | 4.0 | 4.8 | 4.0 | 5.2 | 3.0 |
| Colorado | 6.6 | 4.1 | 6.2 | 4.0 | 4.6 | 3.0 |
| Connecticut | 6.4 | 5.5 | 4.4 | 4.0 | 3.4 | 3.0 |
| Delaware | 11.9 | 8.0 | 9.4 | 4.0 | 7.8 | 3.0 |
| District of Columbia | 17.1 | 10.1 | 13.1 | 4.0 | 11.2 | 3.0 |
| Florida | 6.0 | 4.5 | 4.5 | 4.0 | 5.4 | 3.0 |
| Georgia | 5.1 | 5.3 | 5.7 | 4.0 | 6.2 | 3.0 |
| Hawaii | 8.2 | 5.7 | 6.9 | 4.0 | 6.7 | 3.0 |
| Idaho | 5.4 | 4.1 | 3.0 | 4.0 | 9.7 | 3.0 |
| Illinois | 8.2 | 8.4 | 6.8 | 4.0 | 6.5 | 3.0 |
| Indiana | 3.9 | 4.0 | 4.9 | 4.0 | 4.0 | 3.0 |
| Iowa | 4.5 | 5.3 | 3.4 | 4.0 | 3.7 | 3.0 |
| Kansas | 2.8 | 4.0 | 5.1 | 4.0 | 5.5 | 3.0 |
| Kentucky | 3.6 | 6.1 | 3.4 | 4.0 | 4.1 | 3.0 |
| Louisiana | 6.2 | 6.4 | 5.7 | 4.0 | 5.8 | 3.0 |
| Maine | 4.1 | 5.7 | 4.5 | 4.0 | 4.1 | 3.0 |
| Maryland | 8.2 | 7.2 | 5.3 | 4.0 | 5.7 | 3.0 |
| Massachusetts | 7.4 | 8.0 | 11.4 | 4.0 | 7.8 | 3.0 |
| Michigan | 8.2 | 5.7 | 9.1 | 4.0 | 8.0 | 3.0 |
| Minnesota | 3.0 | 4.0 | 2.6 | 4.0 | 2.0 | 3.0 |
| Mississippi | 4.7 | 6.5 | 3.5 | 4.0 | 2.0 | 3.0 |
| Missouri | 4.8 | 6.0 | 3.4 | 4.0 | 3.7 | 3.0 |
| Montana | 2.5 | 5.9 | 2.5 | 4.0 | 6.9 | 3.0 |
| Nebraska | 9.6 | 4.2 | 4.7 | 4.0 | 6.9 | 3.0 |
| Nevada | 1.3 | 4.0 | 2.7 | 4.0 | 2.1 | 3.0 |
| New Hampshire | 5.9 | 6.3 | 4.3 | 4.0 | 7.5 | 3.0 |
| New Jersey | 7.3 | 5.8 | 6.4 | 4.0 | 5.1 | 3.0 |
| New Mexico | 10.5 | 4.3 | 6.3 | 4.0 | 5.9 | 3.0 |
| New York | 8.0 | 5.6 | 9.4 | 4.0 | 7.1 | 3.0 |
| North Carolina | 3.3 | 5.3 | 2.7 | 4.0 | 3.5 | 3.0 |
| North Dakota | 1.9 | 4.0 | 2.1 | 4.0 | 4.7 | 3.0 |
| Ohio | 7.6 | 5.8 | 5.6 | 4.0 | 6.4 | 3.0 |
| Oklahoma | 3.8 | 4.0 | 4.1 | 4.0 | 3.0 | 3.0 |
| Oregon | 7.1 | 6.9 | 6.0 | 4.0 | 4.6 | 3.0 |
| Pennsylvania | 8.5 | 8.1 | 9.1 | 4.0 | 9.1 | 3.0 |

**Table 7.2** (*cont.*)

|  | 1982 | | 1983 | | 1984 | |
|  | *Error Rates* | *Target Rates* | *Error Rates* | *Target Rates* | *Error Rates* | *Target Rates* |
|---|---|---|---|---|---|---|
| Puerto Rico | 8.9 | 5.3 | 8.6 | 4.0 | 7.7 | 4.0 |
| Rhode Island | 5.7 | 6.9 | 6.2 | 4.0 | 3.7 | 3.0 |
| South Carolina | 8.9 | 5.0 | 7.1 | 4.0 | 7.8 | 3.0 |
| South Dakota | 3.7 | 4.3 | 2.1 | 4.0 | 2.9 | 3.0 |
| Tennessee | 4.9 | 5.0 | 4.5 | 4.0 | 4.3 | 3.0 |
| Texas | 8.4 | 5.0 | 7.2 | 4.0 | 5.7 | 3.0 |
| Utah | 5.0 | 4.0 | 5.7 | 4.0 | 5.8 | 3.0 |
| Vermont | 4.5 | 4.2 | 7.9 | 4.0 | 5.8 | 3.0 |
| Virgin Islands | 4.6 | 6.4 | 8.6 | 4.0 | 2.4 | 4.0 |
| Virginia | 4.1 | 6.6 | 3.8 | 4.0 | 3.5 | 3.0 |
| Washington | 6.4 | 4.9 | 4.8 | 4.0 | 4.1 | 3.0 |
| West Virginia | 8.2 | 6.4 | 3.0 | 4.0 | 4.0 | 3.0 |
| Wisconsin | 6.5 | 6.4 | 5.1 | 4.0 | 6.6 | 3.0 |
| Wyoming | 4.8 | 4.0 | 7.7 | 4.0 | 5.6 | 3.0 |

Source: U.S. Department of Health and Human Services

social entitlements. The potential for administrative redefinition of entitlements is greatest when, as in welfare, statutes are complex and ambiguous.

One lesson of this analysis is that, for programs such as welfare, administrative reform virtually requires making tradeoffs between competing political objectives. Although these tradeoffs may be made on manifestly nonpolitical grounds, as Claus Offe astutely observed, "it is certain that there is no such thing as an administrative reform that is *nothing but* an administrative reform: it always entails changes in the quality of the available social services, their accessibility to clients, the composition of the clientele, and so on" (Offe, 1984, pp. 105–106; emphasis added).

Another lesson to be derived from this analysis is that, not only the content, but also the context of administrative reform bears consideration. The meaning imparted to reform depends, in part, on the political environment within which reformers act and, in part, on the biases of the reformers themselves. Officials in the Nixon Administration and, later, in Congress, defined reform to be consistent with their interests in controlling federal welfare expenditures, in the absence of legislative agreement on a response to the welfare explosion.

In retrospect Joel Handler may have been correct, when in 1973 he advised the Joint Economic Committee of Congress to consider the drawbacks of comprehensive legislative reform as a way to bring efficiency and better management to welfare. He stated that:

If one agrees that the welfare poor are still considered "undeserving" then the poor might very well be better off under the decentralized, inefficient State administrations. . . . This is not a desirable situation since the rules are enforced from time to time, often for unworthy reasons, but it may be a more preferable situation for most recipients than an efficient bureaucracy carrying out harsh rules. Until the day for generous treatment of the poor is at hand, I believe the strategic retreat would be to keep welfare administration complex, working at cross-purposes, and starved for staff (Handler, 1973, p. 35).

Alternatively, in contrast to Handler's pessimistic assessment of comprehensive legislative reform and to other reforms described previously, one may wonder whether administrative reform could be made to work to the advantage of the poor. Technically, one can imagine devising reforms that would implement a liberalization of welfare. Certainly, performance measures could be revised to incorporate protections for the poor, such as those Jerome Mashaw specified in his original blueprint for quality control. His design envisioned reforms that would protect the poor from bureaucratic abuses that abrogated entitlement rights, not reforms that favored errors of stringency over errors of liberality. But, as should be apparent, progressive administrative reform is not merely a technical matter.

Given the current political context, national welfare reform—administrative or legislative—is apt to be decidely unfavorable to the interests of the poor. In that case, those who seek to liberalize welfare policy and its administration might be wise to discourage comprehensive national reform. A more fruitful strategy might concentrate on those states where growing fiscal surpluses, partisan politics, and local-level concerns about feeding the hungry and housing the poor offer a more hospitable political environment for progressive reform.

## Some Larger Implications

Beyond the specifics of administrative welfare reform there are potentially wide-reaching implications in the conversion of policy politics into administrative form. While the case analyzed here is hardly social welfare state politics writ small, it does provide a point of departure for considering some of the larger theoretical problems discussed at the outset of this inquiry.

If there are nonpolitical alternatives to the more conflictual political forms of making welfare state policy, as Offe hypothesized, then neither the breakdown forecast by neo-Marxist "crisis" theory nor the paralysis predicted by pluralist "governability" theory need occur. Deborah Stone provides support for this proposition in her study of disability policy (Stone, 1984). She concludes that contradictory mass democratic demands for social entitlements and the economic requirements of capital accumulation have been accommodated, in part, by changing medical definitions of disability to be more or less inclusive over time. In effect, "flexibility" was re-introduced into the provision of social benefits despite increasing rigidity in the formal definition of entitlement.

But there is something disturbing about "flexibility" achieved through medical redefinition of eligibility (in the disability case) or administrative redefinition (in the case of welfare). Such adaptations constitute, in effect, a reordering of the process of policy politics. It is important, then, to be clear about how that order is achieved.

First, it involves changing the arena and terms of conflict, transferring political conflict from legislative and electoral institutions to administrative agencies. There it is transformed into technical or nonpolitical form. Second, this alternative form of policy politics limits the scope of conflict by depoliticizing it and obscuring the role of administrative agencies in determining its outcome. Third, policymaking, disguised as policy delivery, is rationalized according to managerial criteria, in part through the use of sophisticated technical tools.[13] Fourth, this alternative form avoids political disorder by drawing legitimation from the association of administrative activities with nonpolitical values.

One might say that administration is, in many ways, an appropriate symbolic referent for the nonpolitics of the post-industrial age. As a political symbol, it structures perceptions, invokes commonly shared beliefs, and evokes specific types of reactions. The administrative system, according to Murray Edelman, is a "symbol and ritual which, among other functions, serves as legitimizer of elite objectives" (Edelman, 1964, p. 68).[14] As a symbol, administration is imbued with the attributes of rationality, control, and "neutral competence." It is these attributes that suggest it as an antidote to the disorganized and unmediated political conflict that characterizes ungovernability. Overt attempts to impose order on this system, perhaps through the exercise of centralized authority, are apt to make the society simultaneously more repressive and more unmanageable. However, the indirect ordering of politics and policy through administrative means offers the potential for political control while minimizing the threat of a reaction to that control.

Institutional adaptations to conflict and stalemate, such as the administrative alternative described here, may assume critical importance in the years ahead if analyses of recent events are correct.[15] These analyses suggest that the Reagan Administration, despite its early legislative successes in cutting welfare and other social programs, has also encountered familiar problems symptomatic of continued disorganization in the conflict-resolving institutions of American government. One indication of continuing "ungovernability" is that opposition from the Democratic majority in the House of Representatives to the Republican in the White House has reasserted itself, impeding Administration efforts to advance objectives in a variety of social policy areas. Second, groups that benefit from social welfare programs (other than the poor) have demonstrated that interest group politics still can be effective, at least in blocking major changes in distributive programs. This has been clearest in the case of social security, one of the most expensive federal social welfare programs, whose vocal constituents have beaten back efforts to limit eligibility or retract cost-of-living adjustments.

What this suggests is that welfare policy and welfare state politics, more broadly, are apt to be as contentious as ever in the coming years. Further, the prospect of significant improvement in overtly political means of resolving conflicts is doubtful, barring a major reordering of electoral politics that revitalizes the party system or a crisis of the magnitude of the Great Depression.[16] In these circumstances, the implications of institutional adaptations to political deadlock merit careful consideration.

The case of administrative welfare reform could be interpreted to indicate that adaptations which convert policy politics into nonpolitical form may be functional in overcoming problems associated with ungovernability. But such adaptations would appear, at best, to be temporary "solutions" to ungovernability because they fail to treat its underlying problems. Furthermore, the administrative alternative described here was necessarily indirect and incremental in order to remain relatively invisible. This implies limits on the state's capacity to respond to problems of great magnitude and immediacy.

But even if it is functional, in my view this adaptive form of policy politics is undesirable. I would argue that political order and policy direction achieved by limiting participation and disguising the political agenda is inherently undemocratic. It depends on building a "substitute consensus," which Offe defines as a "consensus that does not result from a democratic process as formally provided for by democratic institutions, but a consensus resulting from informal, highly inaccessible negotiations among poorly legitimized representatives of functional groups" (Offe, 1979, p.10).

It also is worth noting that the historical advancement of European social welfare states was associated generally with organized political participation by groups deriving social benefits from the state.[17] Socialist and labor-based political parties and labor unions gave a relatively strong and sustained voice to advocates of social welfare policies. In contrast, the adaptive form of politics described here functions by excluding from the policymaking process those groups that seek social support from the state. The poor and disadvantaged—who, for now, are without effective champions among elites or organized interests—are apt to be doubly disadvantaged when policy politics is converted into administrative form or when policy is made through informal, bureaucratic means.

Alexis deTocqueville predicted that a political system governed by a dominant middle-class would be ungenerous toward its least successful citizens. The prospect of an ungenerous and begrudging welfare state can only be enhanced by the emergence of political rules-of-the-game that effectively purchase adaptativeness at the price of participation. That is, perhaps, the least promising development for the future of American welfare politics.

# Appendix A

## Quality Control Review Elements

The quality control review of active welfare cases is conducted by state agency reviewers using a standard federal format. Reviewers sample case records and conduct a field investigation, as needed, to document that each AFDC family is eligible for the full amount of its grant. The state level review is guided by a detailed manual of instructions. The accuracy of this review is monitored through a federal re-review of a sample of cases. The index of quality control review elements shown in this appendix (and in use at the time of this study) indicates the types and quantity of details incorporated into the monitoring process.

## ELEMENT AND NATURE OF ERROR CODES*

(Guide for coding Item U on Quality Control Review Schedule)

---
### Basic Program Requirements (100)
---

110...Age.................................................................

120...School attendance...................................................

130...Living with specified relative......................................

          Child(ren) not provided continuing care and supervision (01)...

          Alleged child(ren) non-existent (02).........................

          Required relationship not established (03)....................

Deprivation:

  141...Death................................................

  142...Incapacity...........................................

  143...Continued absence....................................

  144...Unemployed father....................................

          Not unemployed for at least 30 days (04)....................

          Not currently registered with employment agency (05).........

          Employed full-time (06).....................................

          Insufficient quarters of employment coverage (07)............

          Receives unemployment compensation benefits (08).............

          Refuses to accept suitable employment (09)...................

150...WIN program (Talmadge amendment)....................................

          Refuses to participate in WIN program (10)...................

          Failed to register or attend required training (11)..........

          Failed to determine that recipient must register (12).........

          Incorrect exemption determination (13)......................

160...Citizenship and alienage............................................

170...Residence...........................................................

Child support program:

  181...Social security number...............................

  182...Assignment of support...............................

  183...Cooperation in support activity.....................

---
### Resources (200)
---

210...Real property (home and other).......................................

          Exceeds prescribed limits (14)..............................

          Transferred outside agency policy (15)......................

          Lien requirements not met (16)..............................

220...Life insurance......................................................

          Exceeds prescribed limits (14)..............................

          Transferred outside agency policy (15)......................

Liquid assets and personal property:

  231...Bank deposits or cash on hand.......................

          (Nature codes same as for 220...Life insurance).............

  232...Motor vehicle.......................................

          (Nature codes same as for 220...Life insurance).............

  239...Other liquid assets or personal property............

          (Nature codes same as for 220...Life insurance).............

---

*Code 99 is to be used if no statement and code is provided for the nature of the error or if the nature of the error is apparent from the agency or client code.

310...Earned income.....................................................
      Employment status changed from none or part-time to
        full-time (17)..............................................
      Employment status changed from none or full-time to
        part-time (18)..............................................
      Employment status changed from part-time or full-
        time to irregular (19).....................................
      Employment status changed from employed to unemployed (20)....
      Employment status remains the same but earnings
        changed (21)...............................................
      Conversion to monthly amount not used or incorrectly
        applied (22)...............................................
      Averaging not used or incorrectly applied (23)...............
      Allocation not used or incorrectly applied (24)..............
      Other computation error (25).................................
Earned income disregards:
  321...Work incentive exemptions.....................................
  322...Mandatory deductions........................................
      Failed to apply all applicable allowances (26).............
      Failed to use, or incorrectly applied, income tax
        exemptions (27)............................................
      Conversion to monthly amount not used or incorrectly
        applied (22)...............................................
      Other computation error (25)...............................
  323...Work related expenses.......................................
      Failed to apply all applicable allowances (26).............
      Conversion to monthly amount not used or incorrectly
        applied (22)...............................................
      Failed to use, or incorrectly applied, proportionate
        share (28).................................................
      Other computation error (25)...............................
      Expense not incurred or income-in-kind provided (29)........
      Change in amount paid by recipient (30).....................
  324...Child care expenses.........................................
      Allowance exceeds maximum (31).............................
      Allowance less than amount paid by recipient (32)..........
      Conversion to monthly amount not used or incorrectly
        applied (22)...............................................
      Other computation error (25)...............................
      Expense not incurred or income-in-kind provided (29)........
      Change in amount paid by recipient (30).....................
      Recipient pays for item (33)...............................
  329...Other earned income disregards.............................
      (Any appropriate code listed under Earned income disregards)
330...RSDI benefits.................................................
Other pensions or benefits:
  341...Veterans' benefits.........................................
  342...Unemployment compensation.. ...............................
  343...Workmen's compensation.. ..................................
  349...Other (military, railroad retirement, SSI, etc.).............

Other cash income:
    351...Support payments made to Child Support Agency (applicable only
        to ineligible cases)......................................
    352...Contributions.............................. ..... ............
        Conversion to monthly not used or incorrectly applied (22)..
        Averaging not used or incorrectly applied (23).............
        Allocation not used or incorrectly applied (24)............
        Other computation error (25)...............................
    359...Other......................................................
        (Nature codes same as for 352...Contributions).............
    360...Non-earned income disregards (relocation expenses, student loans,
        income set aside for future needs, etc.).....................

Basic budgetary allowance:
    411...Shelter only.............................. ..................
        Failed to use, or incorrectly applied, proportionate
          share (28).............................................
        Expense not incurred or income-in-kind provided (29)........
        Change in amount paid by recipient (30). ..................
        Allowance exceeds maximum (31)..............................
        Allowance less than amount paid by recipient (32)...........
        Recipient pays for item (33)................................
    412...Fuel and/or utilities only (including water and sewer).......
        (Nature codes same as for 411...Shelter)....................
    413...Basic budgetary allowance(s) other than shelter, fuel and
        utilities................................................ .. .....
        (Nature codes same as for 411...Shelter)....................
    414...Shelter combined with fuel and/or utilities..................
        (Nature codes same as for 411...Shelter)....................
    415...Shelter combined with other basic budgetary allowance(s)
        except fuel and/or utilities......... ....................
        (Nature codes same as for 411...Shelter).. ................
    416...All basic budgetary allowances...............................
        (Nature codes same as for 411...Shelter)....................
Special circumstance allowance (non-work related):
    421...Special diet (including pregnancy allowance)..................
        Allowance exceeds maximum (31)..............................
        Allowance less than amount paid by recipient (32)...........
        Special need required (34)............................ .......
        Special need not required (35).......... ...................
    422...Transportation..............................................
        (Nature codes same as for 421...Special diet)...............
    423...Child care..................................................
        (Nature codes same as for 421...Special diet)...............
    429...Other special allowances (including personal care)...........
        (Nature codes same as for 421...Special diet).. ............

## Other  (500)

510...Arithmetic computation........................................
       (This element refers to error in computation of <u>entire</u>
       case budget.  Computation error involving a specific
       element should be coded as a nature code under the
       appropriate element.)....................................
520...Proper person(s) in budget.....................................
       (This element is used <u>only</u> in cases where no other element is
       applicable.)............................................
       Eligible person excluded (36)...........................
       Non-eligible person included (37).......................

# Appendix B

## Massachusetts Quality Assurance Review Document

Quality assurance is the internal, state agency review of case records used to determine procedural errors made at the local office level. Reviewers examine cases that have been redetermined, that is, reassessed for eligibility, by caseworkers. Based on a review of 80 percent of the redeterminations conducted each quarter, quality assurance provides an indicator of case processing accuracy for each welfare office.

The quality assurance review seeks evidence of procedural inconsistencies that are apt to produce quality control errors, which are subject to federal fiscal penalties. It presents detailed definitions of the documentation caseworkers are expected to provide as part of the eligibility assessment process. The document reproduced in this appendix is the one used by the Massachusetts Department of Public Welfare at the time of this study.

QA DOCUMENT

DATE COMPLETED:

Q1.  Region:                              enter number [ ] 1

1 = Boston        4 = Lawrence
2 = Springfield   5 = Greater Boston
3 = Worcester     7 = New Bedford

Q2.  WSO #                                [ ][ ] 2

Q3.  WSO Name:                            [ ][ ][ ][ ][ ][ ][ ][ ]
                                          [ ][ ][ ][ ][ ][ ][ ][ ] 3

Q4.  Case Assignment Number of the Supervisor
     for this case as of the target date:  [ ][ ] 4

     4a.  Supervisor Name:    Last:        [ ][ ][ ][ ][ ][ ] 4a

                              First:       [ ] 4b

Q5.  Social Security Number of Grantee Relative:  [ ][ ][ ][ ][ ][ ][ ][ ][ ]   5

Q6.  Case Name:              Last:         [ ][ ][ ][ ][ ] 6a

                             First:        [ ][ ][ ] 6b

Q7.  Reviewer Name_____#     [ ][ ] 7

Q8.  (Reserved for Quality Assurance)      [ ][ ][ ] 8

Q9.  Type Sample:                          [ ] 9

     1 = Redetermination   2 = QC
              3 = Intake

Q10. Target Date                           [ ][ ][ ][ ][ ][ ] 10
                                           M  M  D  D  Y  Y

Q11. ENUMERATION

     11a. Does the record indicate one or more
          members of the assistance group with-
          out a valid Social Security Number?

          YES = 1   NO = blank (skip to 11d)   [ ] 11a

Q11. ENUMERATION (Cont)

11b. How many members do not have one of the following
acceptable proofs of application for an SSN?

. Form ENUM-2 (Rev. 10/79), signed by SSA

. Form ENUM-2 (Rev. 07/80), signed by SSA

. Social Security Administration Form 5028
filled in by SSA

Enter Number................................. 11b ☐

11c. Indicate whether any such forms are dated more than
90 days prior to the target date.

NO FORMS OVER 90 = blank   5028 ONLY OVER 90 = 2
ENUM-2 ONLY OVER 90 = 1   BOTH ENUM-2 AND 5028
N/A = 8                     OVER 90 = 3.... 11c ☐

11d. Does the information listed on the TD in blocks 5 and 55
accurately reflect the information in the case record?

YES = blank   NO = 1   N/I = 9................. 11d

Q12. BIRTH VERIFICATION AND RELATIONSHIP

12a. Is there birth verification in the case record for all
dependent children receiving AFDC?

YES = blank   NO = 1   N/A = 8............... 12a ☐

12b. Is there valid verification in the case record to prove
relationship between all dependent children and the
grantee relative?

YES = blank   NO = 1   N/A = 8............... 12b ☐

12c. Do TD blocks 16 and 56 on the TD accurately reflect the
information in the case record?

YES = blank   NO = 1   N/I = 9................ 12c ☐

Q13. SCHOOL VERIFICATION

13a. Does the record indicate any children in the assistance
group who are age 18 through 20? ☐ 13a

YES = 1       NO = blank (skip to Q14)

13b. For each such child, is there a statement dated within
45 days prior to the target date verifying school
attendance?

YES = blank   NO = 1........................... 13b ☐

Q13. SCHOOL VERIFICATION  (Cont)

    13c. For each such child who is attending school at least
         half-time  but less than full-time, is there either a
         valid WIN-1 or a communication from DES indicating
         registration or a valid WIN exemption?

                YES = blank   NO = 1   N/A = 8................   13c

Q14. WIN

    14a. Does the record indicate that any mandatory WIN registrant
         in the assistance unit was exempted from WIN registration
         due to illness?

                YES = 1        NO = blank (skip to 14c)........   14a

    14b. For each such person, is the exemption supported by a
         doctor's statement dated within 45 days of the target
         date?

                YES = blank   NO = 1.........................   14b

    14c. Does the record indicate any mandatory WIN registrant in the
         assistance group exempted due to incapacity?

                YES = 1        NO = blank (skip to 14g)........   14c

    14d. For each such person, is the exemption supported by a
         currently valid doctor's statement or verification of
         disability benefits under Title II of Social Security?

                YES = blank   NO = 1 (skip to 14f)............   14d

    14e. Does the valid doctor's statement indicate the in-
         capacity is expected to last 90 days beyond the
         target date?

                YES = blank   NO = 1     NO DOCTOR'S STATE-
                UNABLE TO DETERMINE = 8   MENT = 9........
                                                    14e

    14f. Is there verification of a referral to MRC for each
         such person?

                YES or N/A = blank   NO = 1..................   14f

    14g. Does the case record indicate pregnancy as the sole basis
         of a woman's exemption?

                YES = 1  NO = blank (skip to 14i)   14g

    14h. For each such person, is there a physician's statement
         verifying pregnancy?

                YES = blank   NO = 1.........................   14h

14i. Does the record indicate any children in the assistance group who are age 16 through 17?

        YES = 1      NO = blank (skip to 14k)........   14i

14j. For each such child, is there either: 1) a statement for the current school year dated within 45 days prior to the target date verifying school attendance or, 2) a valid WIN-1 or a communication from DES showing the person is registered?

        1 AND/OR 2 IS PRESENT = blank    N/A = 8   14j
        NEITHER 1 OR 2 IS PRESENT = 1

14k. Does the record indicate the case has been transferred or reopened within the last year?

        YES = 1      NO = blank (skip to 14m)........   14k

14l. For each such case, is there a valid WIN-1, WIN-6 or other DES originated correspondence in the case record dated after the transfer or reopening for each mandatory registrant?

        YES = blank   NO = 1   N/A = 8.............   14l

14m. Is there a valid WIN-1 or a communication from DES indicating registration for all recipients not exempted above or not exempted for other reasons?

        YES = blank   NO = 1   N/A = 8...............   14m

14n. Are the WIN codes listed in blocks 19 and 60 an accurate reflection of information in the case record?

        YES = blank   NO = 1   N/I = 9................   14n

## Q15. CAUSE OF DEPRIVATION

15a. Does the record indicate under/unemployment as the cause of deprivation?

        YES = 1      NO = blank (skip to 15e)........   15a

15b. For any such case, is there verification of application for Unemployment Compensation benefits?

        YES = blank   NO = 1 .........................   15b

15c. Does the unemployed parent meet the work history requirements?

        YES = blank   NO = 1   N/I = 9................   15c

15d. If underemployed, have the work hours been correctly
determined from the paystubs or statement from the
employer?

YES = blank   NO = 1   N/I = 9   N/A = 8............. ....        15d

15e. Does the record indicate incapacity as the cause of
deprivation?

YES = 1          NO = blank (skip to 15i).........         15e

15f. For any such case, is the claim supported by a
currently valid doctor's statement or verification of
SSI DA benefits or disability benefits under Title II
of Social Security?

YES = blank   NO = 1...........................         . 15f

15g. Does the valid doctor's statement indicate the incapacity is expected to last 90 days beyond the
target date?

UNABLE TO DETERMINE = 8    NO DOCTOR'S
YES OR N/A = blank    NO = 1    STATEMENT = 9.....         15g

15h. Is there verification in the case record of the
grantee's application/eligibility for Social Security
benefits?

YES OR N/A = blank    NO = 1....................         15h

15i. Does the record indicate death as the cause of deprivation?

YES = 1          NO = blank (skip to Q16)..........         15i

15j. For any such case, is there verification in the case
record of an application/eligibility for Social
Security benefits?

YES = blank    NO = 1...........................         15j

## Q16. UNEARNED INCOME

16a. Does the record indicate that any person in the assistance
unit receives Social Security benefits?

YES = 1          NO = blank (skip to 16c)..........         16a

16b. For all such persons, have such benefits been verified
on or after the most recent July 2nd?

YES = blank    NO = 1...........................         16b

16c. Does the record indicate any person in the assistance unit
     receives unearned income other than Social Security
     benefits?

            YES = 1        NO = blank (skip to 16e).......... | 16c

     16d. For all such persons, is there verification of each
          such income obtained within 45 days of the target date?

            YES = blank   NO = 1...........................   16d

16e. Does the record indicate there is no cost to the assistance
     unit for rent and    utilities?

            YES = 1        NO  = blank (skip to 16g)......... | 16e

     16f. For any such case, has the appropriate income-in-kind
          figure been deducted from the monthly payment amount?

            YES = blank   NO = 1...........................   16f

16g. Does the information listed on the most current TD in
     blocks 26-29 accurately reflect the information for
     unearned income in the case record?
                                                               16g
            YES = blank   NO = 1   N/I = 9.................

## Q17. BANK DEPOSITS

17a. Does the record indicate that any member of the assistance
     unit (or remarried parent) owns a bank account?

            YES = 1        NO = blank (skip to 18a).......... | 17a

     17b. For all such recipients, have the balances of all bank
          accounts been verified within 45 days of the target
          date?
                                                               17b
            YES = blank   NO = 1...........................

     17c. Has the balance of all bank deposits been applied
          properly to the $1,000 asset limit including the pro-
          rated portion of all accounts owned jointly by the
          grantee (or remarried parent) and third parties?
                                                               17c
            YES = blank   NO = 1   N/I = 9.................

## Q18. HEALTH INSURANCE CODE

18a. Does the health insurance code listed in blocks 31 and 64
     of the TD accurately reflect information in Section 9 of
     the AP-2?
                                                               18a
            YES = blank   NO = 1   N/I = 9.................

Q19. GRANT

19a. Does Section V of the TD accurately reflect the number of eligible dependents noted in the case record?

YES = blank    NO = 1    N/I = 9.................    19a

19b. Does the number of active dependents in Section V, Block 58 of the TD equal the number of dependents listed in Block 21 of the TD?

YES = blank    NO = 1............................    19b

Q20. EARNINGS

20a. Does the record indicate countable earned income for any member of the assistance unit (including the remarried mother)?

YES = 1        NO = blank (skip to end).........    20a

20b. Does the case record contain five paystubs or enough stubs or employer-originated pay records that provide five weeks of information for the current wage calculation?

YES = blank    INCORRECT NUMBER = 1
(complete 20c/20d, skip to end)

NO PAYSTUBS = 2 (skip to end)

UNABLE TO DETERMINE = 9 (skip to end)    20b

20c. Are all the wage verifications used by the worker within six weeks of the date of the home/office visit?

YES = blank (skip to 20e)    NO = 1.............    20c

20d. How many weeks prior to the target date is the earliest day covered by a pay verification used by the worker?

Enter number of weeks............    20d

20e. Are the wage verifications for consecutive weeks?

YES = blank    NO = 1............................    20e

20f. Has eligibility for the standard deduction ($28.00), or prorated share thereof, been correctly determined by the caseworker?

YES = blank    NO = 1............................    20f

20g. Has eligibility for transportation expenses been correctly determined by the caseworker?

YES = blank    NO = 1............................    20g

20h. Has eligibility for other work-related expenses been correctly determined by the caseworker?

                YES = blank    NO = 1............................     20h

HAVE THE FOLLOWING COMPUTATIONS BEEN CORRECTLY PERFORMED?

    20i. Conversion of wages to monthly amount?

                YES = blank    NO = 1............................     20i

    20j. Work Incentive exemption ($30 plus one-third)?

                YES or N/A = blank    NO=1 .....................     20j

    20k. Mandatory payroll deductions?

                YES or N/A = blank    NO = 1....................     20k

    20l. Other work-related expenses? (e.g. Transportation, child care, etc.)

                YES or N/A = blank    NO = 1....................     20l

20m. Resultant countable income correctly subtracted from the monthly payment amount?

                YES = blank    NO = 1............................     20m

20n. Is the information in blocks 26 and 27 of the TD correct?

                YES = blank    NO = 1    N/I = 9................     20n


                                    END


Q21. For Quality Control sample cases only, enter the QC review number. For all other samples, leave blank.     21

# Notes

## Chapter One

1. The expansion that followed the War on Poverty occurred through growth of existing programs, such as AFDC, and the extension of other programs, including food stamps, Medicaid, and supplemental security income. See Weaver (1985) for an analysis of expansionary and restrictive trends in social entitlements. He calculates that the expansionary period ran from about 1965 to 1974.

2. See Chapter Three for a discussion of legislative reform efforts.

3. This term is borrowed from Aaron Wildavsky, who defines *policy politics* as being concerned with the question, "What should policy be?" In contrast, *partisan politics* is concerned with which political party will win office, and *system politics* involves how decision structures will be set up. See Wildavsky (1966), p. 304.

4. Murray Edelman urges greater political attention to these activities. He asserts that "while dramatic, publicized, and controversial political actions wield less and less influence on the quality of people's lives, the thousands of daily bureaucratic actions we take for granted as mere 'implementation' . . . do shape how well we live. The phase of future politics that deserves closest attention is the bureaucracy—the phase we typically see as dull, specialized, and technical, or as the mechanical carrying out of the landmark decisions of the representative branches of government." Edelman (1983), pp. 234–235.

5. This "bottom up" concept of policymaking is elaborated in Chapter Two. Also see Lipsky (1978).

6. Excellent descriptions of the history and growth of public welfare programs in the U.S. may be found in a variety of works on this subject. The brief summary in this section draws primarily on accounts in Bell (1965), Handler and Hollingsworth (1971), Joe and Rogers (1985), Patterson (1981) and Steiner (1971).

7. This definition of deprivation is contained in Title IV of the Social Security Act of 1935.

8. The work incentives permitted $30 plus one-third of earnings to be deducted from household income in calculating AFDC grants. The Omnibus Reconciliation Act of 1981 sharply cut the applicability of this work incentive provision, allowing a family to take earnings deductions for no more than four months.

9. This book does not attempt to assess if, as Piven and Cloward (1971) have argued, changes in welfare policy occur primarily in response to the need of the capitalist political economy to balance upward pressure on wages against the maintenance of social control. Rather, it focuses directly on the mechanisms that permit shifts in policy to occur under particular political conditions. That welfare's growth in the sixties produced a sense of crisis and contraction in the seventies is consistent with Piven and Cloward's argument, but not exclusively so. It is also consistent with

analyses that explain alarm at welfare's growth in terms of ideology and a more general anti-welfare ethic. For an excellent debate of Piven and Cloward's important thesis, see Trattner (1983).

10. Hanson and Berkman (1986) astutely point out that states have been able to contain welfare costs, in part, by failing to make timely adjustments for inflation to payment levels or to the standards of need on which eligibility is based. However, states varied widely in their payment practices, and federal authorities could not count on states to assert control over rising welfare rolls. Some states (for example, California and Indiana) acted in advance of federal pressure to curb welfare, while others (for example, Massachusetts and Michigan) showed little evidence in the early seventies of a concerted interest in or capacity for taking restrictive measures.

11. The acceptable rate of error has been a hotly disputed issue and has varied significantly over the decade of quality control's use, as will be discussed in detail in subsequent chapters.

12. Among these studies are Baker and Vosburgh (1977); Bendick, Lavine, and Campbell (1978); Piliavin, Masters, and Corbett (1979); Zeller (1981); and Mills (1981).

13. For an elaboration of this perspective, see Pressman and Wildavsky's influential analysis (1973).

14. For matters of "fact" rather than opinion asserted by individuals interviewed, I obtained validation from at least one other source or, if possible, by independent documentation. I indicate in the text where ambiguities and uncertainties remained.

## Chapter Two

1. See especially Lowi (1979), Lindblom (1979), and Truman (1951).

2. For elaborations on this theme, see Huntington (1975), Sundquist (1980, 1986), and King (1975).

3. The Sundquist view of government incompetence would appear to be born out by the vast literature on implementation failures.

4. For different elaborations of this view see O'Connor (1973), Piven and Cloward (1971), and Katznelson (1981).

5. Claus Offe points to areas of convergence of the "crisis" theories of the right and left. He asserts that "everyone is convinced of the facts of crisis and . . . general agreement exists regarding its symptoms and course of development." For a thorough analysis of the meaning of these convergences and underlying differences, see Offe (1984), ch. 2, "'Ungovernability': The Renaissance of Conservative Theories of Crisis."

6. The New Deal model is described in Landis (1938), and Ackerman and Hassler (1981), especially chs. 1–2.

7. On these points see, for example, Lax (1978) and Mills (1981).

8. For a thorough analysis, see Lipsky (1980).

9. Courts provide only a partial safeguard, in part because they become involved only if affected parties are aware of informal bureaucratic activities that adversely affect them and have both legal grounds and resources to bring legal action.

Even then, courts are often reluctant to intervene in matters they perceive to be reasonably within the realm of administrative discretion.

10. The effects of common practice at the inspector level need not be adverse, of course. For example, Carol Adaire Jones (1982) (to whom I am indebted for discussing aspects of OSHA enforcement) has found in the case of asbestos that OSHA enforcement practices effectively introduce into policy a balancing between risks and costs that does not exist in formal regulation. Whether this is positive or negative depends on whether one owns the plant or works there. Jones's study indicates that worker exposure to asbestos fibers is higher in plants that have higher costs of compliance with formal standards. Note also that budget and staffing cuts have been an important part of the Reagan Administration's efforts to reduce environmental controls. See Vig and Kraft (1984).

11. Even when political opposition does mobilize around a technical issue, as has occurred in cases of environmental standard setting and risk management, the battle tends to be defined scientifically. Melnick (1983) has found that even when courts appear to have intervened decisively in such cases, they may effectively end up turning the matter back into the hands of the bureaucrats, because they fail to grasp fully the technical issues at stake.

12. For an interesting discussion of the political dimensions of a technical tool, see Thomas and Bailar (1984).

13. Merton's classic elaboration of Parsonian functionalism (1968) distinguishes between the manifest and latent (invisible or unintended) consequences of social structures.

## Chapter Three

1. For an elaboration of the agenda-setting perspective, see Cobb and Elder (1972).

2. For the seminal statement on the significance of the scope of conflict, see Schattschneider (1960). The strategic importance of agenda-setting struggles, he writes, is that "whoever decides what the game is about decides also who can get into the game," p. 105.

3. For a description of social entitlements as "new property rights," see Reich (1964).

4. Murray Edelman (1977) describes the relationship between politics, individual cognition and social constructs in *Political Language*.

5. The theme Long sounded, that the welfare system is infested with "cheats," has been repeated over the decade without notable improvement in methods for evaluating whether cheating is as extensive as it is perceived to be. As one recent report stated, the measures used by federal agencies, including quality control data on "client-caused errors," encompass "everything from mistakes by recipients and bureaucrats to elaborate theft rings by organized crime." Consequently, as this report correctly asserted, "the government can't say with any accuracy how much money it loses each year (Demkovich [1982], p. 1719). Using quality control data, Holmer (1975) estimated fraudulent payments to be between 2 and 5 percent of all AFDC payments. In a more recent study, Gardiner and Lyman (1984) reported that interviews with state officials turned up estimates ranging from 1 to 50 percent.

Despite the ambiguity of their data, the researchers concluded that welfare programs face "substantial problems of fraud and abuse" (pp. 15–16).

6. According to Mashaw, accuracy meant not only making an appropriate judgment relative to available information but also ensuring that the relevant information would be brought before those making decisions (p. 797).

7. According to Marmor and Rein (1973): "The question [for the Nixon Administration] was not what would a reasonable welfare reform plan cost . . . , but what kind of welfare reform was possible within a ceiling then defined as between $2 billion and $3 billion? . . . The origins of this budget constraint are not clear, but its impact was evident in program design. The other important constraint was the necessity of radically changing the AFDC program, or at least appearing to do so. This was of urgent concern because of congressional action taken earlier to curb the size and cost of welfare. States were obliged to accept a work-incentive plan which would raise the earnings level of AFDC eligibility and consequently increase the number of future beneficiaries. These amendments, which went into effect in July 1969, gave urgency to the AFDC reform in early 1969" (pp. 13–14).

8. For further analyses of what went wrong with FAP and the difficulties of forming a coalition around welfare reform, see, in addition to Marmor and Rein (1973), Moynihan (1973), Bowler (1974), and Salamon (1978).

9. For an overview of this strategy, see Nathan (1975).

10. Randall prematurely declared the demise of quality control as an administrative strategy. Although the intentional use of quality control as a political instrument of the Executive may have stopped (temporarily) with the end of the Nixon Administration, its restrictive influence on welfare policy persisted, in part, in response to congressional manipulation of this instrument.

11. For an excellent, detailed review of the features of the quality control system in its early years (pre-1970), see Mills (1981), especially pp. 46–57.

12. Randall points out that when DeGeorge was named associate administrator for management in the Social and Rehabilitation Service in December 1972, he had no social welfare experience. "He came to the welfare programs with a Master of Business Administration degree, a Bachelor of Science degree in accounting, and work experience as a treasurer, vice-president, controller, and cost-accounting manager of several private firms, including divisions of Litton Industries. . . . DeGeorge played a crucial role in the welfare retrenchments during the height of the Nixon campaign to restrict welfare" (p. 802).

13. Sanctions based on error rates offered a more strategic administrative weapon than the "atom bomb" approach of initiating proceedings to disqualify a state from participating in AFDC.

14. Details concerning the negotiations within HEW and between the agency and the states are drawn primarily from Jernigan's (1980) excellent case study. Many of these details were confirmed in my own interviews.

15. Social Welfare advocates were occupied at this point fighting efforts to dismantle the Office of Economic Opportunity. The Welfare Rights Organizations (WROs) had lost much of their organizing power, in part because of administrative decisions to replace special grants with flat grants. The flat grant not only simplified the benefits determination process but also virtually eliminated the major particularistic benefits that WROs could offer prospective members. They had been adept at winning special needs grants and parlaying that skill into an incentive to recipients to join their organizations. See Bailis (1974).

16. According to officials I interviewed, although these reviews were officially resumed in July 1977, in practice they were conducted erratically. Because fiscal sanctions have never been applied to negative errors, they have not been taken very seriously by the states or federal authorities.

17. The requirements that recipients obtain social security numbers and co-operate with child support units were established by the Talmadge Amendment to the Social Security Act of 1976. The purpose of the first requirement was to establish a means of identifying recipients so that computerized cross-checks with various data banks could be made. The second requirement was aimed at making absent fathers help support their families but also may have had more punitive functions, as Piven and Cloward (1971) have noted about a variety of welfare requirements.

18. The income tax credit provided a new means of guaranteeing a minimum income through a relatively simple administrative procedure and, in that respect, was analogous to FAP.

19. The detailed story of the Carter welfare reform proposal is contained in Whitman (1979). See also Califano (1981).

20. Management tools, such as quality control, can be useful in impressing others and minimizing criticism, in this case by helping management "look tough." For other examples, see Sapolsky (1972) and Wildavsky (1979).

21. A UPI story (July 10, 1978) reporting on the public campaign to reduce error begins: "The government yesterday announced a crackdown on fraud and bureaucratic bungling in three welfare programs that it said could save taxpayers $1 billion a year." For the story of this crackdown, see Jernigan (1980), pp. 15–16.

22. These regulations promulgated in March 1979 included a "loophole" that permitted HEW to waive sanctions under broadly specified conditions. According to one participant in the development of the waiver provisions, their inclusion was intended to build on the "good faith" HEW had generated by earlier settling out-standing social service claims. Together, officials hoped that these "good faith" actions would relieve the states' concerns about sanctions and promote accommodation.

23. The "Amendment" was in fact a directive attached to the conference committee's report. Attorneys for the New Coalition were prepared to challenge in court the legality of sanctions based on this directive. Nevertheless, officials at HEW understandably felt compelled to respond as though the directive had the force of legislation. The legality of this directive re-emerged as an issue in 1985 when states became liable for fiscal sanctions based on regulations prepared in accordance with the "Amendment." See Chapter Seven.

24. Although national error rates declined, the urban, high-error states that constituted the largest part of HEW's political problem continued to generate high error rates.

25. Simon (1983) describes quality control as one of a variety of initiatives advocated by social welfare "liberals" to extend entitlement guarantees. However, he concludes that these efforts were "co-opted" and adapted by conservatives with the political goals of restricting eligibility and benefits and disciplining the lower level public workforce (p. 1264–1265).

26. Although, ultimately, both Harris and her successors in the Carter Admin-istration used quality control waiver provisions to avoid imposing sanctions, in 1979 and 1980 states perceived the sanctions threat as credible. (See Chapter Five.) My interviews with officials involved in the sanctions decisions and memoranda made available on a confidential basis indicate that, even at the top levels of HEW, there

was doubt that sanctions could be avoided, primarily because of the political risk of antagonizing powerful congressional opponents by granting waivers extensively.

## Chapter Four

1. This axiom has been examined in a variety of bureaucratic settings. A good review is included in Lipsky (1980), pp. 48–53. For a more general perspective, see Campbell (1975).

2. Certain payment errors do not "count" as errors for quality control purposes. Errors of less than $5 are not counted. Nor are errors that occur because of a change in circumstances that the welfare agency did not pick up within one month. That month is regarded as an "administrative lag" period, effectively giving welfare agencies one month from the time of an actual (if not reported) change to adjust grant payments. Accuracy is determined according to the grantee's circumstances during the designated review month, although the review itself may occur some time later. See Appendix A for a list of the case elements reviewed by quality control.

3. In effect, quality control constitutes an audit of state payments, with fiscal sanctions essentially recouping overpayments. In this sense, quality control in welfare differs fundamentally from the private sector model, which balances concern for product defects against the cost of "perfect" production and which more fully specifies product attributes.

4. HEW does not claim that quality control is a comprehensive performance measure. However, it is the measure for which states are held fiscally accountable.

5. For a full discussion of the threats to measurement validity, see Cook and Campbell (1976), especially pp. 224–246.

6. These difficulties can be ameliorated by careful consideration of alternative causal explanations or, preferably, by the use of multiple measures (Campbell, 1973, p. 200).

7. Consolidated grants appear to reduce measured error but may have a perverse effect with regard to real administrative savings. Depending on the level at which standardized benefits are set, the overall cost of non-targeted benefits may be higher (if more families receive more) or lower (if more families receive less). Politically, a standardized grant that gives most families less is more difficult to implement, at least in the short run.

8. A comprehensive study of this type would be useful to determine more precisely how discretion affects error rate measurement in different states and regions.

9. Workers may receive "tips" from other welfare bureaucrats or from welfare recipients. Workers I interviewed uniformly said that they followed up on tips, even those sent anonymously in the mail.

10. The case record indicated that the mother had given birth in July but that the baby was not added to the family's budget until later that winter. From the documents in the file, it was not possible to establish when the worker was informed of the birth. However, as the case appeared to be otherwise "accurate," further investigation to determine if an underpayment had occurred was not originally considered by the reviewer and subsequently vetoed by the supervisor.

11. State quality control reviewers may be the target of similar tactics on the part of local office workers. One reviewer recounted a favorite story involving his

search for a case that was selected as part of the state sample. Neither clerical staff nor the caseworker could seem to locate the file. On a tip, the reviewer discovered the case record—stashed in a dumbwaiter.

12. Case examples are drawn from documents and interviews. However, names and other details that could identify recipients or workers have been altered.

13. Under certain circumstances, decisionmakers can be expected to respond conservatively when the consequences of their choices are unclear. For a discussion of this point, see Lax and Sebenius (1982).

14. The Child Support Enforcement Unit (CSEU) performs an auxiliary function in the welfare department of searching for absent fathers and seeking payment from them. Mothers are required to cooperate with the CSEU in identifying and locating absent fathers pursuant to the Talmadge Amendment of 1976.

15. Worker responses to notification of a quality control error are closely monitored by a Quality Control Monitoring Unit. Unless a worker disputes an error finding, which is rare, monitors expect the error to be corrected at the local office level. The aggregate impact of this system on workers and clients is relatively minor because of the small number of cases involved.

16. Less than 5 percent of all cases are appealed to fair hearings, and individuals who have difficulty dealing with welfare procedures are the least likely to be able to cope with fair hearing procedures. For a discussion of these points, see Hecker and Nelson (1981), Vesely et al. (1982), and Chapter Six.

## Chapter Five

1. Constraints and boundaries on decisionmaking are not necessarily perceived by the decisionmaker. For a discussion of these terms, see Lindblom (1977) and March and Simon (1958).

2. Administrators can be expected to respond to crises as they are placed on the agenda through external pressures (Weinberg, 1977).

3. According to Lipsky (1978), management has the least influence over the bureaucracy's implementation of public policy when (1) the jobs of those who deliver services or benefits involve a relatively great degree of discretion; (2) choices must be made among multiple objectives or work tasks; and (3) the policy to be implemented involves changes in practice within an established bureaucracy.

4. According to the MDPW, 40 percent of its payment errors for the September 1975 to March 1980 quality control review period were due to the agency's failure to take action on available information (Massachusetts Department of Public Welfare, Oct. 28, 1980, p. 3).

5. Although quality control measured the "paper error" of missing social security numbers, the enumeration requirement was substantively connected to the effort to eliminate "fraud, waste, and abuse." Social security numbers permitted agencies to implement computer matches, for example, comparing bank or tax department employer records with recipient-provided information.

The estimated impact of counting enumeration errors is derived from the difference between state and federal quality control estimates for that review period. The state review excluded and the federal review included enumeration errors. The MDPW's agreement to establish a computer link with the Social Security Administration was part of a bargain struck with federal quality control officials, who had been urging the state to deal with its coming enumeration problem. In return, they conceded to state insistence that a case be regarded as "enumerated" if the record verified that a number had been applied for. Federal reviewers had announced their intention to consider a recipient ineligible if a number was not recorded in the file. However, the federal "grace" period for recording a number in the case record was limited to 90 days (interview, 1982).

6. In fact, this was precisely the type of requirement to which a "good" worker—that is, one who used time effectively—would accord low priority.

7. The MDPW touted its successes in its corrective action plan (Oct. 28, 1980) and announced its intention "to keep this previously lethal error under control." By the review period ending March 1981, enumeration errors had been virtually eliminated, accounting for less than 0.1 percent of the state's error rate.

8. This account was given in an unpublished Legal Services Institute memorandum (Oct. 1, 1980), Jamaica Plain, Mass.

9. These research results were reported in two unpublished MDPW memoranda (Aug. 29 and Sept. 10, 1980).

10. This process had begun earlier but was stepped up and implemented by the Pratt administration.

11. Confinement to the office was generally regarded as a serious punishment, as anyone who has spent time in welfare offices may appreciate.

12. Quality assurance was first developed and used in West Virginia in the mid-seventies.

13. The quality assurance review also targeted the "most costly" errors in transcribing case record information onto forms fed into the department's computer. See Appendix B for the quality assurance guide.

14. HEW had adopted that standard in 1969 to simplify the application process.

15. This story was reported in three separate interviews. Whether or not the details occurred precisely as reported, the *story* clearly had an impact.

16. This interpretation had apparently filtered to the worker level within one month. After sending a recipient to apply for death benefits during a redetermination I observed, the worker told me that he regretted having to do that when he was certain the dependents would not qualify for benefits. However, he said his supervisor would refuse to approve redeterminations unless applications to the Social Security Administration were routinely submitted. He said that he had argued this point the first time a case was returned to him for correction but that he had lost.

17. This is hardly a new concept. In fact, it was effectively applied by the Nixon Administration in its effort to gain control of the HEW bureaucracy. This strategy is elaborated in Derthick (1975), Nathan (1975), and Randall (1979). Although efforts to restructure the MDPW had begun before 1979, they were rapidly advanced by the Pratt administration.

18. Publicly, Pratt said that he resigned after a lengthy dispute with the governor over who would appoint top assistants in the MDPW. Rumors abounded in the department and among regional officials that this was just the tip of an ongoing battle over patronage and, ultimately, control of the department, but Pratt denied that patronage was an issue. See Richard and Collins (Sept. 23, 1980).

19. The regulations were 106 CMR: 302.310, 302.311, 302.130, 301.430, and 302.340.

## Chapter Six

1. In addition, as discussed in Chapter Four, the error rate is too crude a measure to determine the extent to which payment accuracy improved. This is because of the error rate's responsiveness to irrelevant factors and the uncertainties of reviewer judgment.

2. As governor of California, Ronald Reagan did claim that a decline in welfare growth during his administration was due to his program of welfare reform. However, as Levy (1978) later demonstrated, the decline was primarily due to other factors. Mendeloff's (1977) assessment of reform's effects in California discussed earlier, suggested that new procedures also may have contributed to this decline by trading errors of liberality for errors of stringency.

3. See New York State study described in Chapter Seven.

4. Although not included in the error rate used for fiscal sanctions calculations, quality control does provide a crude measure of underpayments. But their fiscal and client impact are relatively trivial compared to erroneous denials and terminations, which are only partially and inconclusively monitored by negative case action reviews. Procedures that discourage eligible applicants are not included in any measures. See Chapter Four for discussion of these points and the question of tradeoffs.

5. Many of the Massachusetts strategies had been developed and tested in other states. For example, West Virginia had developed its quality assurance system several years earlier. One of the first states to create greater uniformity in benefits processing was California, which standardized forms and redesigned worker responsibilities as part of the California Welfare Reform Act enacted under Governor Reagan's administration in 1972. See Mendeloff (1977) and Zeller (1981), especially pp. 33–34.

6. Though the separation of social services and financial assistance functions was not specifically related to the state's error reduction effort, cost control was one purpose of the separation, which was mandated by HEW in 1970. For further discussion, see Zeller (1981), pp. 39–41, and Hoshino (1972).

7. The alternative verifications were listed in 106 CMR 303.120 and 303.210.

8. Lipsky (1980) asserts that the interests of street-level bureaucrats include a "desire to maintain and expand . . . autonomy," p. 19. They may also include a desire to help clients, generally or in particular cases.

9. Quality assurance reviewed between 5,000 and 6,000 cases per month, or about 20 percent of the active caseload.

10. Their psychological distance from workers in the field and from the effects of review decisions on welfare clients is illustrated in an anecdote related by several quality assurance reviewers during my observation of their unit. The story, as told, was that the supervisor of a quality assurance unit had apparently received a threatening message from a telephone caller claiming to be a welfare recipient who had just been notified that his family's benefits were to be terminated on orders from quality assurance. The chief source of amazement among the quality assurance reviewers was that a caseworker would reveal quality assurance decisions to a client and that a client would hold a reviewer personally responsible for the loss of benefits.

11. The emergence of the "45–day rule" to define the "currentness" of verifications is a case in point. See Chapter Five.

12. Telephone lines were often overloaded, messages not received, and mail undelivered. Moreover, workers seeking to avoid tasks that did not contribute to their measured performance would ignore telephone calls or refuse to see clients

who had come to the office. Those tasks were left to the one "duty worker" assigned to handle them for each unit. For further discussion, see Brodkin and Lipsky (1983), p. 35.

13. Asked to estimate the extent to which their clients' procedural difficulties resulted in a loss of benefits, worker estimates ranged from "no problem" to 20 to 30 percent of the clients whose cases they handled.

14. The facts of this case are taken from the legal and administrative records. Names and identifying details have been changed to protect the family's privacy.

15. Ironically, AFDC policy has been rewritten under the Reagan Administration to restrict benefits to the last term of pregnancy.

16. The responsiveness of street-level bureaucrats to their clients is influenced by their assessments of them. In jobs such as that of the financial assistance worker, the "deserving" client tends to be the one who tries and eventually manages to comply with bureaucratic requirements, while others are regarded as "troublemakers." See McCleary (1978).

17. This case was exceptional in its complexity and also presented a variety of legal problems, which are omitted from this discussion because of their confidentiality. Despite the necessity of providing less than a full account of this case, every effort has been made to provide a fair representation of the issues it involved.

18. The advocate in this case explained his decision to send x-rays, which a welfare worker was obviously incompetent to evaluate, as part of an effort to overwhelm the worker with evidence of his client's openness and to try to head off further delays by anticipating new demands.

19. For a discussion of the rationing of presumably available benefits, see Prottas (1981) and Lipsky (1980), especially chs. 7 and 8.

20. Fair hearings, which must be initiated by the recipient, are sought by only a tiny fraction of claimants, less than 5 percent. However, this is rarely taken to suggest that so few claimants are aggrieved. Nor should one assume the direction of bias in this self-selected sample. A review of fair hearings claims in Boston indicates a variable mix of "legitimate" grievances and also many appeals filed by clients who were misinformed or who misunderstood the provisions of welfare policy in fundamental ways. Hecker and Nelson (1981) noted that about 10 percent of the cases they reviewed for each of three years were essentially requests for someone to explain their workers' decisions or to tell the hearing examiner that, right or wrong, their welfare benefits would be inadequate to cover their expenses (p. 45).

21. At Roxbury Crossing, reinstatement rates (cases reopened within one month of closing) in 1980 were as follows: January, 8 percent; February, 6 percent; March, 32 percent; April, 30 percent; May, 31 percent; June, 17 percent; July, 19 percent; August, 19 percent; September, 13 percent; October, 9 percent; November, 19 percent (Recipient Master File, December 1980, MDPW, AFDC).

22. For example, fair hearing data could have provided an initial clue to quality control's systematic effects. Negative case action reviews could have been redesigned to include a full field investigation. Or the department could have collected data on churning as an indicator of procedural obstacles to eligibility.

## Chapter Seven

1. Among the commonly-used cost-cutting devices reported in the APWA survey were: profiling of error-prone cases, increasing the frequency of case rede-

terminations, running computer checks for recipient employment records, and re-organizing office procedures.

2. The NAPA report also discusses the continuing state-level opposition to quality control sanctions. State officials tend to argue that it is too crude a tool for fiscal sanctions and may encourage inefficient investment of administrative resources into "gaming" the system to reduce measured errors.

3. One perverse consequence of inadequate communication with clients occurs when clients complete application forms incorrectly because they are mis-informed. This would result in more administrative errors were it not for the fact that the "cost" of misinformation is passed on to the applicant. Vesely et al. (1982) report an example in which "an applicant included the landlord as a member of the household unit because he lived in the same building, and so was denied assist-ance" (p. 16).

4. A particularly memorable anecdote involved a caseworker's demand for verification that a recipient could not get work as a laborer. The recipient was known by the caseworker to be in a full body cast (Vesely et al., 1982, p. 22).

5. The methodology of the study, which relied largely on case records and fair hearing results, makes it difficult to assess the extent to which proceduralism occurring within the parameters of the regulations may have prevented otherwise eligible families from obtaining aid. For example, the report notes that a requirement for face-to-face recertifications in New York City welfare offices is associated with a high rate of case closings. In practice, closings for non-compliance with this rule failed to distinguish between clients who never received a notice of their appointment and those who chose not to appear because they *believed* they were no longer eligible. That this requirement was not imposed in upstate New York welfare offices, which had a lower closing rate, is subject to various interpretations. It is manifestly explained by higher city error rates. But it bears a certain similarity to Progressive era reforms that established restrictive voting requirements only in regions with large immigrant populations. Whether this was "fraud control" or "electoral control" is arguable. For a fascinating debate of these points, see Burnham (1965) and Converse (1972).

6. Herbert Simon (1969) argues that a system's behavior can be predicted by treating it as if it were operating purposefully.

7. See discussion of the Urban Institute report (Bendick et al., 1978), Chapter Four.

8. In *The Administrative Presidency*, Nathan (1983) argues that administra-tive strategies that permit authoritative action enhance democratic responsiveness. From this perspective, the President is more or less presumed to embody the "public will" or, at minimum, to be politically accountable for his actions.

9. For an account of this furor, see Pear (1983). The Administration's quotas limiting administrative law judges' discretion to overturn erroneous terminations also engendered opposition from Congress and from within the bureaucracy. See also U.S. Congress, House of Representatives, Select Committee on Aging (1982).

10. HHS later waived penalties for six states (Arizona, Maryland, New Jersey, South Carolina, Utah, and Vermont).

11. "Abusing the War on Welfare Abuse," *New York Times*, Oct. 15, 1985, p. A30. See also American Public Welfare Association W-Memo. April 1982. "Re-agan's Bid for Zero Error Rate Encounters Skepticism in the States," p. 1.

12. The increase in the poverty rate experienced since 1980 has not been reflected in higher welfare rolls, as the following figures indicate:

| Year | Poverty Rate (percent) | AFDC Recipients (thousands) |
|------|------------------------|------------------------------|
| 1980 | 13.0 | 10,774 |
| 1981 | 14.0 | 11,079 |
| 1982 | 15.0 | 10,358 |
| 1983 | 15.2 | 10,737 |

Source: Statistical Abstract of the United States, 1985, p. 456.

13. Among those tools are performance measurement, cost-benefit analysis, and risk assessment. However, as Melvin Anshen noted with respect to one technical tool, program budgeting, "the central issue is . . . nothing less than the definition of the ultimate objectives of the Federal government as they are realized through operational decisions" (Anshen, quoted in Wildavsky, 1966, p. 303).

14. The literature on workplace organization as a mechanism of social control takes a different cut at a similar theme. It tends to link organizational developments within firms to their need to assert political control over labor. See, for example, Braverman (1974), Harring (1947), and Edwards (1979). Edwards makes a direct link between problems of "governability" discussed here and organizational structures—both public and private. He asserts that "it is as though capitalists have applied to the state the lessons they learned in the workplace: institutionalized authority replaces more direct—and more directly challenged—rule" (p. 212).

Also, there is a growing body of literature that recognizes administration as a new form of political control. Christopher Lasch has noted a "shift from political to administrative control in which issues allegedly too abstruce and technical for popular understanding fall under the control of professional experts" (Lasch, 1981, p. 32). He points to the growth of a professional civil service, regulatory commissions and government agencies of all types as evidence of this shift. The depoliticization of issues transformed in this way is also alluded to by Lowi, who argues that "administration is rationality applied to social control" (Lowi, 1979, p. 21). "The counterpart to the apolitical citizen," according to Sheldon Wolin, is the "new [managerial] type . . . remarkable for ruling without the appearance of it. The manager combined the professional skill with selflessness, low visibility, and a pronounced aversion to public discourse" (Wolin, 1981, p. 29).

15. For revealing appraisals of the Administration's successes and difficulties in achieving its legislative program, see Greenstein (1983), Palmer and Sawhill (1982, 1984), Salamon and Lund (1984), and Stockman (1986). It is too early to judge to what extent the Reagan Administration may have initiated a long-term trend toward strengthened Presidency and reduced "dead lock." For a different perspective on the persistent (and possibly intensifying) problems of political choice in a "zero sum society," see Lester Thurow (1980).

16. Another alternative, of course, is constitutional reform, as proposed by James Sundquist (1986). However, in order to be enacted, it would have to surmount precisely those political obstacles that it aims to correct. Consequently, Sundquist is led to conclude that "nothing is likely to happen short of crisis" (p. 251).

17. A comparative analysis of social welfare state development is beyond the scope of this book. Among the many excellent treatments of this subject, some of those most pertinent to this specific point can be found in Heclo (1974), Furniss and Tilton (1977), Skocpol and Ikenberry (1983), and Wilensky and Lebeaux (1965).

# Glossary

| | |
|---|---|
| ADC | Aid to Dependent Children |
| AFDC | Aid to Families with Dependent Children |
| CSEU | Child Support Enforcement Unit |
| EA | Emergency assistance |
| Enumeration | The designation of a social security number |
| FAW | Financial assistance worker |
| FAP | Family Assistance Plan |
| Fair hearing | An administrative appeal procedure for welfare clients |
| GAO | U.S. Government Accounting Office |
| HEW | U.S. Department of Health, Education and Welfare (now HHS) |
| HHS | U.S. Department of Health and Human Services (formerly HEW) |
| MDPW | Massachusetts Department of Public Welfare |
| NCA | Negative case action (a decision to deny or terminate welfare benefits) |
| OMB | U.S. Office of Management and Budget |
| OPA | MDPW Office of Program Assessment |
| Quality control | A federal system for monitoring the accuracy of benefits distributed by states in the AFDC, Medicaid, food stamps and SSI programs |
| Quality assurance | MDPW's internal monitoring system that measures the procedural accuracy of case processing in local welfare offices |
| SEIU | Service Employees International Union |
| SRS | U.S. Social and Rehabilitation Service |
| SSA | U.S. Social Security Administration |
| SSI | Supplemental security income |
| WIN | Work incentive program |

# References

Aaron, Henry J. 1973. *Why Is Welfare So Hard to Reform?* Washington, D.C.: Brookings Institution.

Ackerman, Bruce A., and Hassler, William T. 1981. *Clean Coal/Dirty Air*. New Haven, Conn.: Yale University Press.

Allison, Graham T. 1971. *Essence of Decision Explaining the Cuban Missile Crisis*. Boston: Little, Brown.

American Public Welfare Association, National Council of State Public Welfare Administrations. 1981. "A Survey of Income Maintenance Cost-Cutting in State Human Services Agencies." Washington, D.C.

Anderson, Martin. 1978. *Welfare: The Political Economy of Welfare Reform in the United States*. Palo Alto, Calif.: Hoover Institution Press.

———. 1980. "Welfare Reform." In Peter Duignan and Alvin Rabushka, eds. *The United States in the 1980s*. Stanford, Calif.: Hoover Institution Press.

Baer, William C. 1975. "On the Making of Perfect and Beautiful Social Programs." *The Public Interest* 39: 80–98.

Bailis, Lawrence. 1974. *Bread or Justice*. Lexington, Mass.: Lexington Books.

Baker, Timothy, and Vosburgh, W. W. 1977. "Workers, Cases, and Errors: The Effect of Work Load on Errors in Public Assistance Eligibility Determinations." *Administration in Social Work 1:* 161–170.

Bateman, Peter, et al. 1980. *Administration of AFDC in Massachusetts: A Description of Three Local Offices*. Cambridge: Abt Associates.

Baum, Daniel J. 1974. *The Welfare Family and Mass Administrative Justice*. New York: Praeger.

Bell, Daniel. 1976. "The End of American Exceptionalism." In Nathan Glazer and Irving Kristol, eds. *The American Commonwealth—1976*. New York: Basic Books.

Bell, Winifred. 1965. *Aid to Dependent Children*. New York: Columbia University Press.

Bendick, Marc, Jr., Lavine, Abe, and Campbell, Toby H. 1978. *The Anatomy of AFDC Errors*. Washington, D.C.: Urban Institute.

Bowler, M. Kenneth. 1974. *The Nixon Guaranteed Income Proposal*. Cambridge: Ballinger.

Braverman, Harry. 1974. *Labor and Monopoly Capitol*. New York: Monthly Review Press.

Brodkin, Evelyn, and Lipsky, Michael. 1983. "Entitlement Programs at the Local Level: Quality Control in AFDC as an Administrative Strategy." *Social Service Review* 34(4): 22–43.

Brooks, Harvey. 1984. "The Resolution of Technically Intensive Public Policy Disputes." *Science, Technology and Human Values* 9(1):39–50.

Burnham, Walter Dean. 1965. "The Changing Shape of the American Political Universe." *American Political Science Review* 59: 7–28.

———. 1978a. "Great Britain: The Death of the Collectivist Consensus." In Louis Maisel and Joseph Cooper, eds. *Political Parties: Development and Decay.* Beverly Hills, Calif.: Sage Publications.

———. 1978b. "The 1976 Election: Has the Crisis Been Adjourned?" In W. D. Burnham and M. W. Weinberg, eds. *American Politics and Public Policy.* Cambridge: MIT Press.

———. 1980. "American Politics in the 1980s." *Dissent* 27:149–160.

———. 1981. "The 1980 Earthquake: Realignment, Reaction, or What?" In Thomas Ferguson and Joel Rogers, eds. *The Hidden Election.* New York: Pantheon.

———. 1982. "The Eclipse of the Democratic Party." *Democracy* 2(3): 7–17.

Bush, Malcolm, and Gordon, Andrew C. 1978. "Client Choice and Bureaucratic Accountability: Possibilities for Responsiveness in a Social Welfare Bureaucracy." *Journal of Social Issues* 34(4): 22–43.

Califano, Joseph A., Jr. 1981. *Governing America: An Insider's Report from the White House and the Cabinet.* New York: Simon & Schuster.

Campbell, Donald T. 1973. "Reforms as Experiments." In James A. Caporaso and Leslie L. Roos Jr., eds. *Quasi-Experimental Approaches: Testing Theory and Evaluating Policy.* Evanston, Ill.: Northwestern University Press.

———. 1975. "Assessing the Impact of Planned Social Change." In G. M. Lyons, ed. *Social Research and Public Policy.* Hanover, N.H.: Dartmouth College, Public Affairs Center.

Cobb, Roger W., and Elder, Charles D. 1972. *Participation in American Politics: The Dynamics of Agenda-Building.* Baltimore: Johns Hopkins University Press.

Commission on Federal Paperwork. June 10, 1977. *Administrative Reform in Welfare.* Report to the President of the United States.

Converse, Phillip E. 1972. "Change in the American Electorate." In Angus Campbell and Phillip E. Converse, eds. *The Human Meaning of Social Change.* New York: Sage Publications.

Cook, Thomas D., and Campbell, Donald T. 1976. "The Design and Conduct of Quasi-Experiments and True Experiments in Field Settings." In Marvin D. Dunette, ed. *Handbook of Industrial and Organizational Psychology.* Chicago: Rand McNally.

———. 1979. *Quasi-Experimentation Design and Analysis Issues for Field Settings.* Chicago: Rand McNally.

Crenson, Matthew. 1971. *The Un-Politics of Air Pollution: A Study of Non-Decision Making in the Cities.* Baltimore: Johns Hopkins University Press.

Cunningham, Mary. 1977. "Eligibility Procedures for AFDC." *Social Work* 22: 21–26.

Danziger, Sheldon, Haveman, Robert, and Plotnick, Robert. 1980. *Retrenchment or Reorientation: Options for Income Support Policy.* Madison, Wis.: Institute for Research on Poverty, University of Wisconsin.

Demkovich, Linda E. 1982. "Welfare Cheating-Dealing with the Problem and Not with the Image." *National Journal* 14(41): 1719–1722.

Derthick, Martha. 1970. *The Influence of Federal Grants: Public Assistance in Massachusetts.* Cambridge: Harvard University Press.

————. 1972. *New Towns In-Town*. Washington, D.C.: Urban Institute.

————. 1975. *Uncontrollable Spending for Social Services Grants*. Washington, D.C.: Brookings Institution.

Edelman, Murray. 1964. *The Symbolic Uses of Politics*. Urbana, Ill.: University of Illinois Press.

————. 1977. *Political Language*. New York: Academic Press.

————. 1983. "The Future of American Politics." In Mark E. Kann, ed. *The Future of American Democracy*. Philadelphia: Temple University Press.

Edwards, Richard. 1979. *Contested Terrain*. New York: Basic Books.

Elmore, Richard F. 1978. "Organizational Models of Social Program Implementation." *Public Policy* 26(2): 185–228.

————. 1979. "Backward Mapping: Implementation Research and Policy Decisions." *Political Science Quarterly* 94: 601–616.

Elazar, Daniel J. 1962. *The American Partnership*. Chicago: University of Chicago Press.

Friedman, Barry L., and Hausman, Leonard J. 1977. "Welfare in Retreat: A Dilemma for the Federal System." *Public Policy* 25(1): 25–48.

Furniss, Norman and Tilton, Timothy. 1977. *The Case for the Welfare State*. Bloomington, Ind.: Indiana University Press.

Gardiner, John A., and Lyman, Theodore R. 1984. *The Fraud Control Game: Responses to Fraud and Abuse in AFDC and Medicaid Programs*. Bloomington, Ind.: University of Indiana Press.

Gilbert, Charles E. 1975. "Welfare Policy." In Fred I. Greenstein and Nelson W. Polsby, eds. *Handbook of Political Science*, vol. 6. Reading, Mass.: Addison-Wesley.

Gilbert, Neil, and Specht, Harry. 1974. *Dimensions of Social Welfare Policy*. Englewood Cliffs, N.J.: Prentice-Hall.

Goodban, Nancy Ann. 1981. "Attributions: About Poverty." Ph.D. dissertation, Harvard University.

Greenfield, Lawrence, and Friedman, Daniel J. 1978. "Definition of Work-Related Factors in AFDC Decisions." Massachusetts Department of Public Welfare, Office of Research and Evaluation, Boston.

Greenstein, Fred I. 1983. *The Reagan Presidency: An Early Assessment*. Baltimore: Johns Hopkins Press.

Grodzins, Morton. 1966. *The American System*. Chicago: Rand McNally.

Grønbjerg, Kirsten A. 1977. *Mass Society and the Extension of Welfare, 1960–1970*. Chicago: University of Chicago Press.

Grønbjerg, Kirsten A., Street, David, and Suttles, Gerald D. 1978. *Poverty and Social Change*. Chicago: University of Chicago Press.

Handler, Joel F. 1973. "Federal-State Interests in Welfare Administration." In *Studies in Public Welfare, Paper No. 5 (Part 2), Issues in Welfare Administration: Intergovernmental Relationships*. U.S. Congress, Joint Economic Committee. Joint Committee Print, 93rd Cong., 1st sess.

Handler, Joel F., and Hollingsworth, Ellen Jane. 1971. *The "Deserving Poor": A Study of Welfare Administration*. Chicago: Markham.

Hanson, Russell L. and Michael B. Berkman. 1986. "Containing the 'Welfare Explosion': Strategic Action in a Federal System." Paper presented at the Annual Meeting of the Western Political Science Association, Eugene, Or.

Hargrove, Erwin. 1978. "Implementation." *Policy Studies Journal* 5: 9–15.

Harring, Sidney. 1947. *Policing a Class Society: The Experience of American Cities, 1865–1915.* New Brunswick, N.J.: Rutgers University Press.

Hartz, Louis, ed. 1964. *The Founding of New Societies.* New York: Harcourt, Brace, and World.

Haveman, Robert H. 1977. "Poverty, Income Distribution, and Social Policy: The Last Decade and the Next." *Public Policy* 25(1): 3–24.

Hecker, Betsy, and Nelson, Teresa. 1981. "AFDC Fair Hearings: A Study of Administrative Due Process." Unpublished manuscript, Legal Services Institute, Jamaica Plain, Mass.

Helco, Hugh. 1974. *Modern Social Politics in Britain and Sweden: From Relief to Income Maintenance.* New Haven, Conn.: Yale University Press.

Holmer, Martin. 1975. "The Economic and Political Causes of the 'Welfare Crisis.'" Ph.D. dissertation, Massachusetts Institute of Technology.

Hoshino, George. 1972. "Separating Maintenance from Social Services." *Public Welfare* 30: 54–61.

Huntington, Samuel P. 1973. "Congressional Responses to the 20th Century." In David P. Truman, ed. *Congress and America's Future,* 2nd ed. Englewood Cliffs, N.J.: Prentice-Hall.

———. 1975. "The United States." In Michel Crozier, Samuel P. Huntington, and Joji Watanuki, eds. *The Crisis of Democracy.* New York: New York University Press.

———. 1976. "The Democratic Distemper." In Nathan Glazer and Irving Kristol, eds. *The American Commonwealth—1976.* New York: Basic Books.

Ingram, Helen. 1977. "Policy Implementation Through Bargaining: The Case of Federal Grants-in-Aid." *Public Policy* 25(4): 501–526.

Jernigan, David. 1980. "Controlling AFDC Error Rates." (Parts A-B.) Harvard University, Kennedy School of Government Case Program, C94/80/302–3.

Joe, Tom and Cheryl Rogers. 1985. *By the Few for the Few.* Lexington, Mass.: Lexington Books.

Jones, Bryan D., et al. 1978. "Service Delivery Rules and the Distribution of Local Government Services: Three Detroit Bureaucracies." *Journal of Politics,* 40(2): 332–368.

Jones, Carol Adaire. 1982. "Regulatory Standards: The Cost/Benefit Critique Revisited." Paper presented at the Association for Public Policy and Management Conference, Minneapolis.

Jones, Charles O., and Thomas, Robert D., eds. 1976. *Public Policy Making in a Federal System.* Beverly Hills, Calif.: Sage.

Jordan, Peter. 1981. *Corrective Action and AFDC Dynamics: An Empirical Study in Six Jurisdictions.* Boston: Public Assistance Data Analysis Laboratory, Social Welfare Research Institute, Boston College.

Katznelson, Ira. 1976. "The Crisis of the Capitalist City: Urban Politics and Social Control." In Willis Hawley et al., eds. *Theoretical Perspectives on Urban Politics.* Englewood Cliffs, N.J.: Prentice-Hall.

———. 1981. "A Radical Departure? Social Welfare and the Election." In Thomas Ferguson and Joel Rogers, eds. *The Hidden Election.* New York: Pantheon.

Kennedy, Duncan. 1976. "Form and Substance in Private Law Adjudication." *Harvard Law Review* 89(8): 1685–1778.

King, Anthony. 1975. "Overload: Problems of Governing in the 1970s." *Political Studies* 23(2): 162–174.

————. 1978. "The American Polity in the Late 1970s: Building Coalitions in the Sand." In A. King, ed. *The New American Political System*. Washington, D.C.: American Enterprise Institute.

Landis, James M. 1938. *The Administrative Process*. New Haven, Conn.: Yale University Press.

Lasch, Christopher. 1981. "Democracy and the 'Crisis of Confidence.'" *Democracy* 1(1): 25–40.

Lax, David. 1978. "Measuring Judicial Performance." Unpublished manuscript, Harvard University.

Lax, David A., and Sebenius, James K. 1982. "Negotiating Through an Agent." Working Paper, Graduate School of Business Administration, Harvard University.

Levy, Frank. 1978. "What Ronald Reagan Can Teach the United States About Welfare Reform." In W. D. Burnham and M. W. Weinberg, eds. *American Politics and Public Policy*. Cambridge: MIT Press.

Levy, Frank, Meltsner, Arnold, and Wildavsky, Aaron. 1974. *Urban Outcomes: Schools, Streets and Libraries*. Berkeley, Calif.: University of California Press.

Lindblom, Charles E. 1977. *Politics and Markets*. New York: Basic Books.

————. 1979. "Still Muddling, Not Yet Through." *Public Administration Review* 39(6): 517–526.

Lindsey, Robert. Feb. 27, 1983. "California Weighs Plans to Curb Welfare Fraud." *New York Times*, p. 26.

Lipsky, Michael. 1978. "Standing the Study of Public Policy Implementation on Its Head." In W. D. Burnham and M. W. Weinberg, eds. *American Politics and Public Policy*. Cambridge: MIT Press.

————. 1980. *Street-Level Bureaucracy: The Dilemmas of Individuals in Public Services*. New York: Russell Sage Foundation.

Lockard, Duane. 1976. *The Perverted Priorities of American Politics*, 2nd ed. New York: Macmillan.

Lowi, Theodore J. 1979. *The End of Liberalism: The Second Republic of the United States*, 2nd ed. New York: W. W. Norton.

Lowi, Theodore J., and Stone, Alan, eds. 1978. *Nationalizing Government: Public Policies in America*. Beverly Hills, Calif.: Sage.

Lurie, Irene. 1973. "Legislative, Administrative and Judicial Changes in the AFDC Program, 1967–71." In *Studies in Public Welfare, Paper No. 5 (Part 2), Issues in Welfare Administration: Intergovernmental Relationship*. U.S. Congress, Joint Economic Committee. Joint Committee Print, 93rd Cong., 1st sess.

Marando, Vincent L. 1980. *AFDC Error Rate Case Study: A Small County in Georgia*. Washington, D.C.: National Academy of Public Administration.

March, James G., and Olson, Johan P. 1983. "Organizing Political Life: What Administrative Reorganization Tells Us About Government." *American Political Science Review* 77(2): 281–296.

March, James G., and Simon, Herbert A. 1958. *Organizations*. New York: John Wiley & Sons.

Marmor, Theodore R., ed. 1971. *Poverty Policy*. Chicago: Aldine Publishing.

Marmor, Theodore R., and Rein, Martin. 1973. "Reforming the Welfare Mess: The Fate of the Family Assistance Plan, 1969–72." In Allan P. Sindler, ed. *Policy and Politics in America*. Boston: Little, Brown.

Marris, Peter, and Rein, Martin. 1973. *The Dilemmas of Social Reform.* Chicago: Aldine Publishing.

Mashaw, Jerry L. 1974. "The Management Side of Due Process." *Cornell Law Review, 59:* 772–837.

Massachusetts Department of Public Welfare. Jan. 1978. "AFDC Corrective Action Plan." Unpublished report to the U.S. Department of Health, Education and Welfare.

———. Sept. 1979. "Quality Assurance." Unpublished internal memorandum.

———. Jan. 21, 1980. "AFDC Quality Control Statistical Analysis." Unpublished document.

———. Feb. 15, 1980. Unpublished memorandum to assistance payment staff (AP-ADM-80-5).

———. Oct. 28, 1980. "Corrective Action Plan: Aid to Families with Dependent Children." Unpublished report to the U.S. Department of Health and Human Services.

———. July 30, 1981. "AFDC and GR Caseload Report: April-June 1981." Unpublished report to the Massachusetts General Court, House and Senate Committees on Ways and Means.

McCleary, Richard. 1978. "On Becoming a Client." *Journal of Social Issues 34*(4): 57–75.

McDonald, Thomas P., and Piliavin, Irving. 1984. "Failure to Participate in AFDC: Some Correlates and Possible Influences." *Social Work Research and Abstracts, 20*(3): 17–22.

McLanahan, Sara. 1980. "Organizational Issues in U.S. Health Policy Implementation—Participation, Discretion and Accountability." *Journal of Applied Behavior 16*(3): 354–369.

Melnick, R. Shep. 1983. *Regulation and the Courts: The Case of the Clean Air Act.* Washington, D.C.: Brookings Institution.

Mendeloff, John. 1977. "Welfare Procedures and Error Rates: An Alternative Perspective." *Policy Analysis 3*(3): 357–374.

Merton, Robert K. 1968. *Social Theory and Social Structure,* 2nd ed. New York: Free Press.

Miller, S. M., and Roby, Pamela A. 1970. *The Future of Inequality.* New York: Basic Books.

Mills, Gregory. 1981. "Quality Control in Welfare Administration: An Analysis of Payment Error in AFDC." Ph.D. dissertation, Harvard University.

Moynihan, Daniel P. 1973. *The Politics of a Guaranteed Income.* New York: Random House.

Murphy, Jerome. 1974. *State Education Agencies and Discretionary Funds.* Lexington, Mass.: D. C. Heath.

Nathan, Richard P. 1975. *The Plot That Failed: Nixon and the Administrative Presidency.* New York: John Wiley & Sons.

———. 1983. *The Administrative Presidency.* New York: John Wiley & Sons.

Newton, Robert D. 1978. "Administrative Federalism." *Public Administration Review 38*(3): 252–255.

New York State Department of Social Services. 1984. "Administrative Closings of New York City Public Assistance Cases." Unpublished report.

Nivola, Pietro. 1978. "Distributing a Municipal Service: A Case Study of Housing Inspection." *Journal of Politics 41*(1): 59–81.

Nonet, Philippe. 1969. *Administrative Justice: Advocacy and Change in a Government Agency.* New York: Russell Sage Foundation.

Nordlinger, Eric. 1981. *On the Autonomy of the Democratic State.* Cambridge: Harvard University Press.

Oates, Wallace E., ed. 1977. *The Political Economy of Fiscal Federalism.* Lexington, Mass.: D. C. Heath.

O'Connor, James. 1973. *The Fiscal Crisis of the State.* New York: St. Martin's Press.

Offe, Claus. 1979. "The State, Ungovernability and the Search for the 'Non-Political.'" Paper presented at the Conference on the Individual and the State, Toronto, Canada.

———. 1984. *Contradictions of the Welfare State.* Cambridge: MIT Press.

Palmer, John L. and Sawhill, Isabel V., eds. 1982. *The Reagan Experiment.* Washington, D.C.: Urban Institute.

———. 1984. *The Reagan Record.* Washington, D.C.: Urban Institute.

Patterson, James. 1981. *America's Struggle Against Poverty, 1900–1980.* Cambridge: Harvard University Press.

Pear, Robert. June 7, 1983. "U. S. Plans to Ease Disability Criteria in Social Security." *New York Times,* p. 1.

Pesso, Tana. 1978. "Local Welfare Offices: Managing the Intake Process." *Public Policy 26:* 305–330.

Piliavin, Irving, Masters, Stan, and Corbett, Tom. 1979. "Administrative and Organizational Influences on AFDC Case Decision Errors: An Empirical Analysis." Discussion Paper 542–79. Madison, Wis.: Institute for Research on Poverty, University of Wisconsin.

Piven, Frances Fox, and Cloward, Richard A. 1971. *Regulating the Poor: The Functions of Public Welfare.* New York: Pantheon.

———. 1981. *The New Class War.* New York: Pantheon.

———. 1982. "Economic Demands, Political Rights." *Democracy 2*(3): 33–41.

Pratt, John D. 1981. "State Agencies Can Be Managed: The Massachusetts Experience with Reducing AFDC Error Rates." *New England Journal of Human Services 1*(2): 20–26.

Pressman, Jeffrey, and Wildavsky, Aaron. 1973. *Implementation.* Berkeley, Calif.: University of California Press.

Price, David A. 1981. *Study of AFDC Cases Discontinued by the Colorado Monthly Reporting System.* Princeton, N.J.: Mathematica Policy Research.

Prottas, Jeffrey. 1981. "The Cost of Free Services: Organizational Impediments to Access to Public Services." *Public Administration Review 41*(5): 526–534.

Randall, Ronald. 1979. "Presidential Power Versus Bureaucratic Intransigence: The Influence of the Nixon Administration on Welfare Policy." *American Political Science Review 73:* 795–810.

Redford, Emmette S. 1969. *Democracy in the Administrative State.* New York: Oxford University Press.

Reich, Charles A. 1964. "The New Property." *Yale Law Journal 73*(5): 733–787.

Rein, Martin, and Heclo, Hugh. 1973. "What Welfare Crisis?—A Comparison Among the United States, Britain, and Sweden." *The Public Interest 1*(33): 61–83.

Rein, Martin, and Rabinovitz, Francine. 1978. "Implementation: A Theoretical Perspective." In W. D. Burnham and M. W. Weinberg, eds. *American Politics and Public Policy.* Cambridge: MIT Press.

Rein, Martin, and Rainwater, Lee. 1978. "The Future of the Welfare State." Paper presented at the IX World Congress of Sociology, Uppsala, Sweden.

Report of the Commission on Federal Paperwork. June 10, 1977. *Administrative Reform in Welfare*. Washington, D.C.: Government Printing Office.

Richard, Ray and Collins, Laurence. September 13, 1980. "State Welfare Head Quits," *The Boston Globe*, p. 1.

Rosenblatt, Rand E. 1982. "Legal Entitlement and Welfare Benefits." In David Kairys, ed. *The Politics of Law: A Progressive Critique*. New York: Pantheon.

Sabatier, Paul, and Mazmanian, Daniel. 1980. "The Implementation of Public Policy." *Policy Studies Journal* 8: 538–560.

Salamon, Lester. 1978. *Welfare: The Elusive Consensus*. New York: Praeger.

Salamon, Lester M. and Lund, Michael S., eds. 1984. *The Reagan Presidency and the Governing of America*. Washington, D.C.: Urban Institute.

Sapolsky, Harvey. 1972. *The Polaris Missile System*. Cambridge: Harvard University Press.

Sard, Barbara. 1982. "Verification Problems in AFDC and GR." Unpublished memorandum, Massachusetts Law Reform Institute, Boston.

Schattschneider, E. E. 1960. *The Semi-Sovereign People*. New York: Holt, Rinehart and Winston.

Shapiro, Harvey D. 1978. "Welfare Reform Revisited—President Jimmy Carter's Program for Better Jobs and Income." In L. Salamon, ed. *Welfare: The Elusive Consensus*. New York: Praeger.

Simon, Herbert. 1969. *The Sciences of the Artificial*. Cambridge: MIT Press.

Simon, William. 1983. "Legality, Bureaucracy, and Class in the Welfare System." *Yale Law Journal* 92(7): 1198–1269.

Skocpol, Theda and Ikenberry, John. 1983. "The Political Formation of the American Welfare State in Historical and Comparative Perspective," in *Comparative Social Research*, 6: 87–148.

Sosin, Michael. 1979. "Social Welfare and Organizational Society." *Social Service Review* 55(3): 392–405.

Steiner, Gilbert. 1966. *Social Insecurity: The Politics of Welfare*. New York: Rand McNally.

———. 1971. *The State of Welfare*. Washington, D.C.: Brookings Institution.

Steinmetz, Daniel. 1980. *Quality Control Errors in the AFDC Program in Michigan: A Case Study*. Washington, D.C.: National Academy of Public Administration.

Stenberg, Carl W. 1981. "Beyond the Days of Wine and Roses: Intergovernmental Management in a Cutback Environment." *Public Administration Review* 41(1): 10–20.

Stern, Sol. 1974. "Welfare Cops, Computer Cards, and Chaos: Making the Poor Pay." In Edwin Schurr, ed. *The Poverty Establishment*. Englewood Cliffs, N.J.: Prentice-Hall.

Stewart, Richard B. 1975. "The Reformation of American Administrative Law." *Harvard Law Review* 88(8): 1667–1813.

Stockman, David. 1986. *The Triumph of Politics: How the Reagan Revolution Failed*. New York: Harper & Row.

Stone, Deborah A. 1984. *The Disabled State*. Philadelphia: Temple University Press.

Street, David, Martin, George T., Jr., and Gordon, Laura Kramer. 1979. *The Welfare Industry*. Beverly Hills, Calif.: Sage.

Sundquist, James L. 1980. "The Crisis of Competence in Our National Government." *Political Science Quarterly* 95(7): 183–208.

———. 1986. *Constitutional Reform and Effective Government*. Washington, D.C.: Brookings Institution.

Thomas, Stephen R., and Bailar, John C., III. 1984. "What Are We Doing When

We Say We're Doing Risk Analysis?" Paper presented at the Annual Conference of the Association for Public Policy Analysis and Management, New Orleans.

Thompson, Frank J. 1981. *Health Policy and Bureaucracy: Politics and Implementation.* Cambridge: MIT Press.

Thurow, Lester. 1980. *The Zero-Sum Society.* New York: Basic Books.

Touche Ross and Company. Oct. 21, 1977. *Evaluation of AFDC-QC Corrective Action.* Final Report and Technical Appendix. Washington, D.C.

Trattner, Walter F., ed. 1983. *Social Welfare or Social Control?* Knoxville, Tenn.: University of Tennessee Press.

Truman, David. 1951. *The Governmental Process: Political Interests and Public Opinion.* New York: Alfred A. Knopf.

U.S. Congress, Congressional Research Service. April 1977. *Administration of the AFDC Program: A Report to the Committee on Government Operations.* Washington, D.C.: Government Printing Office.

U.S. Congress, General Accounting Office. 1977. *Legislation Needed to Improve Program for Reducing Erroneous Welfare Payments.* Washington, D.C.: Government Printing Office.

———. 1979. *Welfare Payments Reduced: An Improved Method for Detecting Erroneous Welfare Payments.* Washington, D.C.: Government Printing Office.

———. 1980. *Better Management Information Can Be Obtained from the Quality Control System Used in the Aid to Families with Dependent Children Program.* Washington, D.C.: Government Printing Office.

———. 1982. *Analysis of Four States Administration of the AFDC Program: Management Improving But More Needs to Be Done.* Washington, D.C.: Government Printing Office.

U.S. Congress, House of Representatives. 1974. *Review of AFDC Program, Hearings Before a Committee on Ways and Means,* 93rd Cong., 2nd sess.

———. Committee on Ways and Means. 1979. *Social Security Administrative Law Judges: Survey and Issue Paper.* Committee Print, 96th Cong., 1st sess. Washington, D.C.: Government Accounting Office.

———. 1982. *Background Material and Data on Major Programs Within the Jurisdiction of the Committee on Ways and Means.* Committee Print, 97th Cong., 2nd sess.

———. Select Committee on Aging. 1982. *Impact of the Accelerated Review Process on Cessations and Denials in the Social Security Disability Insurance Program.*

U.S. Congress, Joint Economic Committee. 1972a. *Problems in Administration of Public Welfare Programs, Hearings Before a Subcommittee of the Joint Economic Committee.* 92nd Cong., 2nd sess.

———. 1972b. *Issues in Welfare Administration: Welfare—An Administrative Nightmare.* Paper No. 5, Part 2. Joint Committee Print, 92nd Cong., 2nd sess. Washington, D.C.: Government Printing Office.

U.S. Congress, Senate, Committee on Finance. 1972. *Welfare Cheating: Address of Hon. Russell B. Long.* Committee Print, 92nd Cong., 2nd sess., March.

———. 1979. *Waste and Abuse in Social Security Act Programs, Hearings Before the Subcommittee on Public Assistance.* 96th Cong., 1st sess.

U.S. Department of Health, Education and Welfare, Office of the Inspector General. March 31, 1978. *Annual Report: April 1, 1977–December 31, 1977.* Washington, D.C.: Government Printing Office.

U.S. Department of Health, Education and Welfare, Region VI Office of Service Delivery Assessment. Jan. 15, 1979. "Service Delivery Assessment of AFDC Negative Case Actions." Unpublished report.

U.S. Department of Health, Education and Welfare, Social and Rehabilitation Service. 1975. *How They Do It: Fraud Control, California and New York.* Washington, D.C.: Government Printing Office.

U.S. Department of Health, Education and Welfare, Social Security Administration. 1978. *Quality Control in AFDC: Case Review Process.* QC Manual/3000. Washington, D.C.: Government Printing Office.

U.S. Department of Health and Human Services, Social Security Administration. 1980. *Social Security Bulletin: Annual Statistical Supplement, 1977–1979.* Washington, D.C.: Government Printing Office.

Van Meter, Donald, and Van Horn, Carl. 1974. "The Policy Implementation Process: A Conceptual Framework." *Administration and Society* 6: 445–488.

Vesely, Marie, McEntee, Sheila, and Schorr, Alvin L. 1982. "Fair Play: A Report of a Study of the Administration of AFDC in Several Midwestern States." Unpublished report, School of Applied Social Sciences, Case Western Reserve University.

Vig, Norman, J., and Kraft, Michael E., eds. 1984. *Environmental Policy in the 1980's.* Washington, D.C.: Congressional Quarterly, Inc.

Weatherly, Richard. 1980. *The Pursuit of AFDC Error Reduction in Washington State.* Washington, D.C.: National Academy of Public Administration.

Weaver, R. Kent. 1985. "Controlling Entitlements." In John E. Chubb and Paul E. Peterson, eds. *The New Direction in American Politics.* Washington, D.C.: Brookings Institution.

Weinberg, Martha Wagner. 1977. *Managing the State.* Cambridge: MIT Press.

Werner, Alan. 1980. *The Management of AFDC in Massachusetts: A Case Study.* Washington, D.C.: National Academy of Public Administration.

Whitman, David. 1979. "The Carter Administration and Welfare Reform" (Parts A-D and Sequel). Harvard University, Kennedy School of Government Case Program, C15/79/238–241.

———. 1980. "Fraud, Abuse and Waste at HEW." Harvard University, Kennedy School of Government Case Program, C14/80/337.

Wildavsky, Aaron. December 1966. "The Political Economy of Efficiency: Cost-Benefit Analysis, Systems Analysis, and Program Budgeting." *Public Administration Review* 26(4): 292–310.

———. 1979. *Speaking Truth to Power: The Art and Craft of Policy Analysis.* Boston: Little, Brown.

Wilensky, Harold L. and Lebeaux, Charles N. 1965. *Industrial Society and Social Welfare.* New York: Free Press.

Witte, John F. 1980. *Welfare Errors in the State of Wisconsin.* Washington, D.C.: National Academy of Public Administration.

Wolin, Sheldon S. 1981. "The People's Two Bodies." *Democracy* 1 (Jan.): 9–24.

Zashin, Elliot, and Summers, Scott. 1980. *Case Processing and Error Rates in the Illinois AFDC Program.* Washington, D.C.: National Academy of Public Administration.

Zeller, Florence. 1981. *AFDC Payment Error Rate Case Studies: Comparative Analysis.* Washington, D.C.: National Academy of Public Administration.

# Index

61–62, 68–69; Operation Perform, 65–67, 81; personnel changes, 75–76; policy clarification, 68–70; WIN errors, 62, 78. *See also* Massachusetts Department of Public Welfare, reform of; Quality assurance

Massachusetts Department of Social Services, 67, 75, 85, 132n12

Mathews, Sec. F. David, 32

MDPW. *See* Massachusetts Department of Public Welfare

Michel Amendment: 36–39, 60, 106, 133n23. *See also* Fiscal sanctions; Quality control

Michel, Sen. Robert, 36–39, 60

Mills, Rep. Wilbur, 29

Monthly reporting, 96

Morrill, William, 32

National Association of Counties, 32

National Conference of State Legislatures, 32

National Governors' Conference, 32

National League of Cities, 32

Negative case actions: case closings in Massachusetts, 79, 89; case closings in New York City, 103, 139n5; churning, 98, 138n21; denials in Massachusetts, 96–98; review process, 33, 43–44

New Coalition, 32–33, 35–36, 133n23

New York City, welfare system, 103, 139n5

Nixon Adminstration, 22–23, 27–29, 33–34

Omnibus Reconciliation Act of 1981, 121n8

O'Neill, Paul, 30

Operation Perform, 65–76, 81

"Paper errors." *See* Massachusetts Department of Public Welfare, reform strategy of: enumeration errors, WIN errors

Performance measurement: discretion in, 57; effects of, 41, 47–48; purposes of, 70; quotas as, 64, 66, 70–71, 75, 86–87. *See also* Quality assurance, Quality control

Policymaking process: models of, 11, 15–17, 19–22; participation in, 21–22

Policy politics: adminstrative alternative to, 4–5, 13, 21–23, 104–106, 107–112; boundaries of, 24; definition of, 4, 112n3

Political symbolism, 104, 105, 111

Poverty: attitudes toward, 5–7, 105–106; rates of, 108, 139–140n12

Pratt, Commr. John D., Jr.: adminstration of, 61–62, 65, 69, 70, 136nn9, 16; background of, 60; claims of, 78, 79, 98; resignation of, 76, 136n17

Professionalism: in social work, 61, 75, 81, 84–85; in welfare, 77

Project Fair Play, 102

Quality assurance: background of, 70–72; effects of, 85, 88; penalties in, 74–75; policy interpretation by, 72–74, 81–82; reviewer attitudes in, 83–84, 137n10. *See also* Performance measurement

Quality control: cooptation of, 133n25; description of, 9–10, 44, 134n3; development of, 26–27, 29–33, 103–104; litigation concerning, 32–33, 43, 106; Michel Amendment to, 36–39, 60, 106, 133n23; political perspective on, 103–104; research on, 44–49, 101, 106; state uses of, 61, 66, 71–72, 104. *See also* Error rates; Fiscal sanctions; Massachusetts Department of Public Welfare, reform strategy of; Quality control process; Quality control regulations

Quality control process: case examples, 53–56; description, 42, 50–52, 71; "gaming the system," 52, 134–135n11, 139n2

Quality control regulations: litigation of, 32–33, 43, 106; proposed in 1970, 30; proposed in 1973, 31–32;